TRANSITIONS

50 DAYS OF WORSHIP

JASON HEIM

BENDED KNEE BOOKS
Levittown, Pennsylvania

Library of Congress Control Number: 2015904709

DEDICATION

I dedicate this book to my children: Taylor, Gibson, Jaylea, Trinity, Parker and Asher whom I pray will surpass their father in dedication, love, and worship of our glorious God.

CONTENTS

INTRODUCTION

A S I READ through the Psalms, I recognize I am a far cry from David. David is, of course, the hero of every worship leader who strives to be a person after God's heart. Unlike David, I am not naturally self-reflective. I am usually content sailing through life without getting in touch with my "inner self." Paul's statement in 1 Corinthians 4:4 fits me well: "My conscience is clear, but that does not make me innocent." I am a "glass half full" kind of guy, and although I am aware of my sinful desires, I usually have a clear conscience. However, as I read the Psalms, I recognize how insincere my worship can be at times.

For most of my life, I dreamed of making it big in the music world. I became a worship pastor in 1996, and I started my own band soon after beginning full-time ministry. We recorded a demo CD and took a trip to Nashville, hoping to get discovered. When that didn't happen, we played in local Christian coffee houses and churches for a few years. But once marriage and children became a priority, I set aside my contemporary Christian music dreams.

A few years later, iTunes came on the scene, and independent worship music was readily available. While I enjoyed the many, talented indie worship leaders I discovered, unfortunately, I also came to the realization that my own musical talent and songwriting skills were far inferior to most of what I was hearing. I realized that if these extremely talented artists could not get signed, there was little hope for me.

Of course, I could have taken the opposite tack. To keep the dream alive and pump myself up, I could have listened to the many inferior bands that have somehow been signed by major Christian record labels, shook my head, and wondered what the executives were thinking. I could have imagined my meeting with a record executive, him telling me that I had a one in a million shot of making it, and then responding in the words of Lloyd Christmas: "So you're telling me there's a chance... Yeah!" Instead, I decided to abandon my Christian music dream completely.

While studying the Psalms, I was struck by the fact that David did not write with the hope of producing marketable songs. He wrote out of the overflow of his heart. Consider Psalm 9, for example. As the title indicates, it was written "for the director of music. To the tune of 'The Death of the Son.' A psalm of David." Sounds like a lively tune! Listen to verse 6: "Endless ruin has overtaken my enemies, you have uprooted their cities; even the memory of them has perished." Do you sing anything like that in your church? I'm not sure this would go over very well in my church. However, David was not interested in what was saleable. All he was doing was pouring his heart out to God.

As I reflected on this, I realized *that* is the kind of worshipper I want to be. I want to start writing songs again, not necessarily to sing in church or release on iTunes but simply to worship God. I probably won't start with a song about the destruction of my enemies, but I want to express God's worth with my own words. As much as I enjoy singing other people's lyrics and making them my heart's cry, I realize I need to express my own thoughts to God in worship. I want to sing like my four-year-old daughter, who, throughout the day, sings songs of worship she creates on the fly. I want to be a worship leader, not just a band member, a song leader, or a wannabe rock star. I want to be a man after God's own heart.

Worship vs. Performance

As I sat down at my desk one Monday morning, I read the following note: "We all know you are very talented, but we do not come to church to see your band perform but to worship God."

Ahhh... the church bulletin comment card. What a brilliant idea! Almost as good as worship band uniforms. Can you feel the sarcasm oozing out of these words? The bulletin comment card was definitely not created by a worship pastor.

Needless to say, this particular comment struck a chord, so to speak, because the last thing I want to be accused of as a worship leader is performing. Our attitude in private must be consistent with what we portray on stage or in the pew.

We have a lot of very talented song leaders in our churches today but not enough worship leaders. Worship leaders cannot lead people to a place they've never been or to a destination they are not seeking themselves. All worship leaders must be good worshippers. If we are not worshiping God in the solitude of our homes when no one is looking, then we are simply singers when we join the multitudes each Sunday. The purpose of this book is to help us become worshippers instead of singers and worship

I believe we should use the talents God has given us to the best of our ability, but for his glory, not our own. We sing to an audience of One!

leaders instead of song leaders. In the process, I hope it will renew your desire to declare the majesty and the wonder of our incredible God, whether you're on your own or leading a congregation of thousands.

The entire congregation should be an extension of the worship leader, band, or choir. Therefore, a lack of participation during a church service is a big problem. Of course, the outward expression, or lack thereof, during worship is not always indicative a worshipper's heart. Some worshippers may simply have a contemplative spirit or participate quietly through their hurt and pain. But participation in some capacity is necessary for worship to be authentic. Unfortunately, many of us are often distracted by the busyness of life or the cares of this world. I have had the opportunity to brainstorm with other worship pastors about how to encourage more people to participate in worship, specifically through music. Many ideas have been tossed around, from singing more of the old hymns to dimming the lights to singing acapella. Some of these ideas may be valid in certain contexts. However, I believe the most effective way to encourage God's people to worship is to remind them continually why we worship. I believe worship leaders need not only to teach by example but also to teach a theology of worship. That second part might sound boring, but hopefully in the following pages you will see this concept is actually very exciting.

This concept might sound like a no-brainer, but I have rarely seen a worship leader, even professionals serving in the biggest churches in the country, do this well. Most worship leaders tend to focus simply on how to enhance the musical experience. As a result, the musical portion of worship in many of our services has become nothing but mindless repetition. This is evident when the expressions on people's faces do not match the words they are singing.

I am not knocking the idea of worshipping through music, but I believe worship leaders need to help people turn off their "screen savers" and focus on Jesus as we engage our minds and hearts in worship. To do this, we need to take a few minutes to remind ourselves why we worship and take opportunities to express our worship using non-musical methods. Worship begins in the heart on a daily basis. If we aren't tuned in to God throughout the week, we won't hear him on Sunday, and we won't be able to help others hear him either.

What is Worship?

Sadly, most Christians relegate "worship" to a half an hour on Sunday morning. As I've indicated above, true worship is not limited to the Sunday morning tradition. It is far, far bigger.

I use the word *worship* about 400 times in this book, so I believe it is important for you to understand what I mean by this word. Likely, whatever comes to mind when you think of worship is actually just a snapshot of the big picture. Your snapshot definition of worship might include music, adoration, praise, sacrifice, obedience, or doing the hipster head bob in your car while listening to Hillsong. These can all be forms of worship, and yet, each expression fails to encompass the whole of worship. In this book, I have elected to use the word *worship* to describe the individual snapshots as well as the entire panorama of praise. Therefore, my big picture definition of worship is *our total response to God in faith.*

I'm Not a Worship Leader—Am I Wasting My Time With This Book?

No! This book is for all worshippers, not just worship leaders or pastors, because God is seeking people of all kinds who are willing to become even more "undignified" for the sake of bringing honor to our Lord Jesus Christ. As a worship pastor, I have used these devotionals to prepare the hearts of all sorts of worshipers to transition into a song of worship, hence the title, *Transitions*. However, I want these devotionals to transcend the simple segue between songs in church and inspire you to transition from a singer into to a worshipper in every aspect of life. My hope is that this book will not only help worship leaders stimulate authentic worship on Sunday mornings but also that the average worshiper will use it as a devotional resource throughout the week.

Allow the stories, Scripture passages, and songs to inspire you to draw close to God each day of the week. And remember, worship is a decision, not just an emotion.

This devotional is designed to be interactive, so don't simply rush through it so you can check it off your to-do list. I've included a number of questions to help you reflect on the theme of each devotional and draw closer to God. Don't skip over them. Take time to reflect on the questions and record your answers in the spaces provided. I've also included worship songs in each devotional, so make sure to choose a song or two and lift your voice to the One who is worthy of worship Monday through Saturday as well as on Sunday.

You will only get as much out of this devotional as you put into it.

If you are not familiar with some of the songs, I encourage you to search for the lyrics online and pray the words out loud. Remember, the Psalms did not include sheet music. The lyrical content and the authentic expression of the worshipper are every bit as important as the tune. So let your worship rise to our Savior even if you don't know the tune. Finally, if you play an instrument, you can find the chord charts for the worship songs that accompany each devotional at www.TransitionsWorship.com.

May God bless you as you seek his face in worship!

50 DAYS OF WORSHIP

DAY 1

Sincerity Versus Obedience

FIRST CHRONICLES 13 contains a magnificent description of a worship service, directed by one of the greatest worship leaders of all time. As you read this account, imagine yourself standing on the hillside observing the nine-mile procession as it makes its way from Abinadab's house toward Jerusalem.

They moved the ark of God from Abinadab's house on a new cart, with Uzzah and Ahio guiding it. David and all the Israelites were celebrating with all their might before God, with songs and with harps, lyres, tambourines, cymbals and trumpets. (v. 7–8)

What would it have been like to experience such a service? I have had the privilege of participating in some lively worship services at the Creation Festival, Battle Cry events, Chris Tomlin concerts, Promise Keepers, and so on, but I am not sure I have ever experienced God's people worshipping "with all their might." In fact, I cannot think of too many experiences in life where I have used all my might. (Actually, my mother-in-law asked me to open a jar of pickles the other week, so that is the closest I have come to using all my might recently.) The question is, what would "pickle-jar-power" worship look like? The worship service described above sounds amazing, but do you know the rest of the story?

> When they came to the threshing floor of Kidon, Uzzah reached out his hand to steady the ark, because the oxen stumbled. The LORD's anger burned against Uzzah, and he struck him down because he had put his hand on the ark. So he died there before God. Then David was angry because the LORD's wrath had broken out against Uzzah... David was afraid of God that day and asked, 'How can I ever bring the ark of God to me?' he did not take the ark to be with him in the City of David. Instead, he took it aside to the house of Obed-Edom the Gittite. (v. 9–13)

I guess it would sort of put a damper on your Sunday morning worship service if God struck one of your worship leaders dead. David, Uzzah, and the other Israelites seemed to have the best of intentions as they worshipped God, so why didn't God accept their worship? Why did God strike Uzzah dead? Take a moment to jot down your answer.

_____

_____

_____

_____

"If at first you don't succeed..." must have been David's motto, because three months later, he gave it another shot. Again, imagine you have a bird's-eye-view of this worship service.

Now King David was told, "The LORD has blessed the household of Obed-Edom and everything he has, because of the ark of God." So David went down and brought up the ark of God from the house of Obed-Edom to the City of David with rejoicing. When those who were carrying the ark of the LORD had taken six steps, he sacrificed a bull and a fattened calf. David, wearing a linen ephod, danced before the LORD with all his might, while he and the entire house of Israel brought up the ark of the LORD with shouts and the sound of trumpets. (2 Samuel 6:12–15)

What are some similarities between this worship service and the first one?

_____

_____

_____

_____

The most striking parallel to me is the description of David worshipping with all his might. Did you observe anything else?

I imagine that if we were actually able to observe both of these worship services—without knowing the ending and all of the theological considerations Scripture brings to light—we would not have noticed too many differences. Each service is described using similar imagery, yet one service was pleasing to God and the other was not. The difference between a worship service that pleases God and one that does not boils down to one word: obedience.

Why isn't sincerity enough? Simple: we can be sincerely wrong about all sorts of things. Have the reverse threads on a toilet's flush lever, the

It seems the worshippers in both services had the best of intentions, but clearly, good intentions are not enough.

nut of the left bicycle pedal, an oxygen tank, or those Wallflower fragrance plugs from Bath & Body Works ever messed with your mind? No matter how hard you try to unscrew them, you only manage to accomplish the opposite of what you intended. Similarly, God would much rather receive our obedience than misguided sincerity. David's mistake was to worship God however he saw fit instead of making sure his heart was in tune with God's Word.

Where did David get the idea to transport the Ark on a cart pulled by oxen? Read 1 Samuel 5–6 and then write down your answer.

_____

_____

_____

_____

David was worshipping God by following the example set forth by God's enemies, the Philistines. Exodus 25:13–15 indicates that the Levites were to carry the Ark using poles (see also Numbers 7:6–9).

This story illustrates that we need to approach God with a humble attitude, seeking forgiveness for when we fall short of his standard for worship, especially when our good intentions lead us astray.

Transition Through Reflection...

What should your goal be in worship?

_____

_____

_____

_____

The goal of our worship should never be just to sing a few songs to Jesus on a Sunday morning. When we gather as a body of believers to sing God's praise, our worship should well up and overflow from a life lived in obedience to our Lord throughout the week. Sincerity is no substitute for obedience. The Father seeks those who worship in Spirit and in truth (John 4:23). Sincerity is an essential element of worship, but it must be coupled with obedience.

Is your worship pleasing to God because you strive to live a life of obedience and trust God's commands (even when you disagree with them), or is your worship simply hype and emotionalism? If you have fallen short of God's standard for worship this week, confess your sin to the One who "is faithful and just and will forgive us our sins and purify us from all unrighteousness" (1 John 1:9).

Suggested Songs

As a way of expressing your desire to worship God in obedience, sing "Heart of Worship" by Matt Redman. You can also sing "Everyday" by Joel Houston of Hillsong, "You're Worthy Of My Praise" by David Ruis, or the hymn "When We Walk With The Lord (Trust And Obey) by Daniel Brink Towner and John Henry Sammis. (Chord charts are available at www. TransitionsWorship.com).

DAY 2

A Doorman In God's Kingdom

(Inspired by Pastor Mike Jarrell of Fellowship Bible Church in Philadelphia, PA.)

YOU PROBABLY REGARD 1 Chronicles as the exciting book that contains the history of King David's reign over Israel. Even so, in your devotions, you likely skipped or skimmed the first nine chapters, which are nothing but genealogies.

However, we can learn some interesting things from these genealogies. One example comes from 1 Chronicles 9. This chapter contains a list of Levites who served at the tabernacle.

> These were the gatekeepers belonging to the camp of the Levites. Shallum son of Kore, the son of Ebiasaph, the son of Korah, and his fellow gatekeepers from his family (the Korahites) were responsible for guarding the thresholds of the Tent just as their fathers had been

responsible for guarding the entrance to the dwelling of the LORD. (v. 18–19)

Most of these names are not familiar to me, but I do recognize the patriarch of the family, Korah, because he is mentioned in another biblical account. Korah was a Levite and a gatekeeper for the tabernacle. Numbers 16 relates the history of this Israelite leader:

> Korah… [and others] became insolent and rose up against Moses. With them were 250 Israelite men, well-known community leaders who had been appointed members of the council. They came as a group to oppose Moses and Aaron and said to them, "You have gone too far! The whole community is holy, every one of them, and the LORD is with them. Why then do you set yourselves above the LORD's assembly?" (v. 1–3)

Korah and his followers had come forward to lodge a complaint against Moses and Aaron. I am sure this kind of thing never happens in your church! If it does, I am certain those who complain are simply defending God's integrity from power-hungry leaders, right?

Good leaders welcome constructive criticism, but we need to remember that simply complaining is sinful (Philippians 2:14). Did you notice Korah's talent in couching his complaints with the most impressive spiritual overtones? "The whole community is holy… and the LORD is with them." That sounds so spiritual and selfless, but what is the essence of Korah's complaint? Moses sheds some light on the nature of it starting in verse 8.

Moses also said to Korah, "Now listen, you Levites! Isn't it enough for you that the God of Israel has separated you from the rest of the Israelite community and brought you near himself to do the work at the LORD's tabernacle and to stand before the community and minister to them? He has brought you and all your fellow Levites near himself, but now you are trying to get the priesthood too."

It turns out Korah's complaint is not really about God's relationship with the Israelite community at all. Instead, he and his fellow gatekeepers are dissatisfied with their role in the tabernacle system of worship. They feel that standing guard all day and opening and closing gates for the priests is beneath them. They want the more prestigious role of priest, where they can receive the recognition they feel they deserve. Pause for a moment and read the remainder of Numbers 16.

In response to Korah's complaint, Moses instructed Aaron and Korah, along with his followers, to gather in front of the tabernacle and offer incense to God. Then God would judge between them. As Korah and his followers offered their incense, the ground opened up and swallowed every man, their families, and all of their possessions.

Interestingly, in Exodus 6:18, 20–21 we find that Korah was Moses and Aaron's first cousin. Jesus said in Mark 6:4, "A prophet is not without honor except in his own town, among his relatives and in his own home." Often the most insidious and hurtful attacks come from those who are part of our inner circle. Our family members and close friends certainly have the potential to wound us far worse than acquaintances and outsiders, because they know us best, and we care about their opinion the most. Therefore, it is important to be vigilant regarding the way we treat friends and family members who open their hearts to us, knowing that we have tremendous power to build them up or tear them down.

Moses told Korah that it was a tremendous privilege to be a doorkeeper in God's tabernacle. Are you a stay-at-home mom? Thank God that you are a servant in his kingdom. Are you the guy who spreads salt on your church sidewalk when it snows? Praise God for the privilege of serving him. Are you the person responsible to change the message on the church sign? No matter what your job, shouldn't you be satisfied with simply having a role, no matter what it is?

Wouldn't it be a privilege to be a janitor in God's kingdom? How about a doorkeeper? Are you satisfied with your role in God's kingdom right now?

To see a completely different attitude from Korah's, read Psalm 84:1–2,10. (I've printed the verse here, but if possible, open your Bible and read the actual text):

How lovely is your dwelling place, O LORD Almighty!
My soul yearns, even faints, for the courts of the LORD;
my heart and my flesh cry out for the living God.
    Better is one day in your courts than a thousand
elsewhere; I would rather be a doorkeeper in the house
of my God than dwell in the tents of the wicked.

If you have your Bible open, scan to the top to find out who wrote this Psalm. That's right, the sons of Korah! The patriarch of their family thought that being a doorman was beneath him, but some of Korah's sons stood against him and said they would rather be servants in God's kingdom than kings in any other context.

Transition Through Reflection...

Often, like Korah, we become discontent with our position in the kingdom and are tempted to seek glory for ourselves. We fall into this state, because we forget that everything we do should be for the purpose of glorifying God, not ourselves. John 3:30 says, "He must become greater; I must become less." That is worship. Do your actions match up with these words? Are you satisfied being a doorkeeper in God's kingdom? List a few "doorkeeper" responsibilities that you are willing to initiate or continue as part of your total response to God in faith.

Initiate:

1. _____

2. _____

3. _____

4. _____

Continue:

1. _____

2. _____

3. _____

4. _____

Suggested Songs

Sing "Better Is One Day" by Matt Redman as a prayer of confession and commitment. If hymns are more your thing, sing "Take My Life And Let It Be" by Frances Ridley Havergal and Henri Abraham Cesar Malan. (Chord charts are available at www.TransitionsWorship.com).

DAY 3
The Flower Child

MY WIFE TRIES to keep our house looking nice and neat, but with five children, it can be a daunting task. It seems like the kids can't help but leave chaos in their wake, taking mere minutes to undo the order that was painstakingly accomplished through significant time and effort. It's even more of a losing battle, because my wife, Leah, is more of an outdoor person. She prefers to work in the yard, so in the spring, she spends much of her time spreading mulch, pulling weeds, and planting flowers.

The boys usually allow the daffodils to complete their natural life cycle in peace, but not the girls. Little girls seem to have this instinctive addiction to pick flowers. Now, this can be beneficial when they mistake dandelions for flowers, as they often do. My girls are always handing me dandelions in the spring, saying, "Daddy, I found this and want you to have it." However, when they pick the flowers my wife planted to create a beautiful accent for our house, things can get ugly fast. Our little girls find themselves on lockdown so they can address their addiction in "flower-picking rehab," better known as "time-out." Is it clear enough that my wife does not appreciate people defiling her garden?

Even so, I can imagine my four-year-old daughter strolling through the yard in the rain without a care in the world. As she rounds the corner, she notices the freshly planted flowers and wonders to herself, "Wow, how did those flowers just pop out of the ground so suddenly?" Of course, she can't resist the temptation to pick one or two or a handful. She carries the flowers into the kitchen, tracking mud from one end of the newly washed tile floor to the other. She reaches up and, in her sweet voice, declares, "Here, Mama, for you!" What mom would not scoop that little girl up in her arms and hug her as long as possible, messy boots and all?

I think this is what our worship looks like from God's perspective. We take the life that God has given us, and we mess it up. We dirty our hands and feet with sinful living, tracking our grime and filth into God's presence, and then we lift our hands and say, "Here, Daddy, this is for you." Only in his mercy does he say, "Thank you! I'll accept your worship. I'll accept your love."

Transition Through Reflection...

Isaiah 64:6b says, "All our righteous acts are like filthy rags." We have messed up God's garden, and yet still he loves us and accepts us. John 6:37b says, "Whoever comes to me I will never drive away." What are some ways that you may have overestimated the quality of your worship?

Spend a few minutes reflecting on and confessing how your worship falls miserably short of God's standard. Then thank him for accepting you anyway.

On our own, we cannot possibly please God. Apart from Jesus, everything we do is filthy, according to the verse you read above. Our motivations and attitudes are always selfish and sinful apart from Christ. Read John 15:1–17. God is pruning his garden and pulling out the dead branches that bear no fruit. Does your life bear fruit? If so, how?

_____

_____

_____

_____

If you don't know what that fruit looks like, read Galatians 5:22–23. Worship is offering God the fruit of your life that is only possible to produce when you are connected to the Vine. God is weeding his garden, and he is working on your area today, so listen as the Holy Spirit reveals what needs to change. He loves you so much that he is willing to enter into your mess.

> Worship is not simply singing a few songs on a Sunday morning; it is living the promises and truth of those songs in everyday life.

To make this really practical, take a few minutes to clean up an area of your house, and then keep an eye out for the first person to mess it up. Give him or her a big hug as you remember how Jesus loves you despite the chaos you spread in his world.

Suggested Songs

Sing "Give Us Clean Hands" by Charlie Hall. You can also sing "Children of God" by David Carr, Mac Powell, Mark D. Lee, and Tai Anderson of Third Day; or the hymns "Nothing But The Blood Of Jesus" by Robert Lowry; "Jesus Paid It All" by Elvina Mabel Hall and John Thomas Grape; or "Just As I Am" by Charlotte Elliott and William Batchelder Bradbury. (Chord charts are available at www.TransitionsWorship.com).

50 DAYS OF WORSHIP

DAY 4

Amazing Grace

"AMAZING GRACE" IS certainly the most well-known worship song in modern history. Even many atheists can sing the lyrics to this song. However, it is probably also one of the most misunderstood songs in Christianity.

John Newton penned the words of "Amazing Grace" in 1773. The first recording of the song was produced in 1926. Jerry Bailey, executive at Broadcast Music, Inc. said, "It may be the most recorded song on the planet." Despite its popularity, few people comprehend what the song is about. In fact, a survey of British teenagers revealed that a majority thought it was a love song about a girl named Grace! Instead, it's a love song written to a Father by one of his children, who had wandered off. But even more tragic than our misunderstandings about the song is that most people don't understand the concept of grace.

My dad is the typical grandparent who spoils his grandchildren. When my oldest son Taylor was born, Dad wanted to come up with his own grandpop nickname. He wanted something original. We already had a "Pop-pop," and we agreed that both "Grandpa" and "Grandfather" were too formal, so he decided he wanted to be called "Lollipop." Please allow me to set the record straight: This is *not* the same man with whom I grew up. My brother, sister, and I also had a nickname for my dad when we were kids, but it was not "Lollipop." It was "Old Yeller."

Befitting his new nickname, from time to time Dad will call us and ask if he can take our kids to their favorite hangout: Chuck E. Cheese's. Not too long ago, I received such a call. Dad explained that he was planning to take my niece to Chuck E. Cheese's, and he invited my kids and me to join him. He continued his invitation by offering the following explanation for this special outing: "Originally, I was going to take her swimming, but she got in trouble and was not allowed to go swimming."

I couldn't believe my ears. So the punishment was going to Chuck E. Cheese's?

That's grace!

Grace is when you deserve a time out, but you get Chuck E. Cheese's instead. Grace is getting what you don't deserve, and if you don't deserve it, there's no way you can earn it.

Ephesians 2:8–9 reads, "For it is by grace you have been saved, through faith—and this not from yourselves, it is the gift of God—not by works, so that no one can boast." In our case, we deserve an eternal "time out" in hell, but not only did Jesus pay our debt by dying on the cross, he also makes us co-heirs with him. Romans 8:17 reads, "Now if we are children, then we are heirs—heirs of God and co-heirs with Christ, if indeed we share in his sufferings in order that we may also share in his glory."

Grace. You can't buy it, you can't earn it, and you can't be good enough to receive it. The only thing you can do is accept it. This is why we call it "amazing"! Lift your voice and sing this well-known anthem of God's goodness.

Transition Through Reflection...

Think back to a time when you experienced grace. If you cannot think of an example, simply consider the last gift you received. Who gave you something you didn't deserve?

_____

_____

Why didn't you deserve the gift?

_____

_____

_____

_____

The answer to the last question is not dependent on your particular situation. Instead, the answer is found within the question itself. If you deserved something, then it does not qualify as a gift. By definition, a gift is unearned and undeserved. If you earned something, then it is a wage, not a gift. Read Ephesians 2:1–9. How is God's grace similar to the example of grace you just considered?

_____

_____

_____

_____

How is it different?

_____
_____
_____
_____
_____

What can you do to repay God for his gift of amazing grace?

_____
_____
_____
_____
_____

This last one is a trick question. Did you catch it? We do not worship in order to repay God for his goodness to us. Instead, our worship is simply a response of gratitude for God's grace.

Take five minutes to make a list of twenty examples of God's grace in your life. Reflect on how amazing his grace is and express your appreciation to God. When you see the list of twenty lines below, you may think you could never fill all that space. However, just get started, and I guarantee that you will breeze through it quicker than you expect.

1. _____
_____

2. _____
_____

3. _____
_____

4. _____

5. _____

6. _____

7. _____

8. _____

9. _____

10. _____

11. _____

12. _____

13. _____

14. _____

15. _____

16. _____

17. _____

18. _____

19. _____

_____

20. _____

_____

Suggested Songs

In addition to "Amazing Grace," you can also sing "You Are My King (Amazing Love)" by Billy J. Foote (popularized by the Newsboys and Chris Tomlin) or the hymn "And Can It Be" by Charles Wesley and Thomas Campbell. (Chord charts are available at www.TransitionsWorship.com).

50 DAYS OF WORSHIP

DAY 5

Star Registry

AROUND CHRISTMAS TIME, I usually hear commercials on the radio for something called a "Star Registry." That's right, you can actually name a real star after someone as a gift. It's perfect for the person on your list who has everything. The ad tugs at your heart with the slogan "Give them the stars!" but it tugs at your wallet with a hefty $54 price tag. Actually, the sentimental side of me loves this gift idea. To have a star named after me or a loved one seems like a really cool idea. However, you should consider a few facts before you lay down some cash.

The Bible indicates that the number of stars in the universe is incredible. God makes a promise to Abraham in Genesis 22:17, saying, "I will surely bless you and make your descendants as numerous as the stars in the sky and as the sand on the seashore." Jeremiah also indicates that the stars are countless (33:22). Even so, throughout history, most scientists and astronomers have assumed a relatively small number of stars.

In 128 BC, Hipparchus, who is known as one of the greatest ancient astronomers, tried to count the stars, and he arrived at an estimate of 1,026. In AD 1600, Johannes Kepler, a mathematician, astronomer, and Christian, performed a recount of the stars, because he believed Hipparchus' estimate was too high. Kepler concluded that there were about 1,005 stars in the universe.

Modern day scientists have finally caught up with the truth—which was written in the Scriptures thousands of years before the technology was available to verify the claim—that the number of stars in the universe is astronomical (no pun intended). Astronomers estimate that the actual number is close to 70 sextillion, which, when written out in numeric form is 70,000,000,000,000,000,000,000. That seems like a pretty large quantity of stars, but because we cannot comprehend numbers that big, we are still prone to downplay the immensity of that figure, so maybe the following comparison will help.

Each summer, my family usually spends some time at the Jersey Shore. In Ocean City, you can stand on the shore and observe beaches full of sand as far as the eye can see in either direction. Would you be impressed if I told you the number of stars in our universe is equivalent to the number of grains of sand on the Jersey Shore? What if I told you the quantity of stars is comparable to the number of grains of sand on the entire east coast of the United States, from Sand Beach in Maine all the way down to Miami? Would you find that amazing? Then consider this: In actuality, scientists have estimated that the number of stars in the universe is comparable to the number of grains of sand on every beach and every desert on the face of the entire planet!

Did you catch what God said to Abraham in Genesis 22:17? He indicates that the number of stars and the number of grains of sand are similar in quantity. How could Moses have possibly known that when he wrote the book of Genesis if it took until now for scientists to verify this? The answer is easy. The One who created it all inspired Moses to include details that were beyond the scope of observation. Therefore, shouldn't we trust his Word as truth even when our best and brightest disagree? Truly, David had it right when he said,

> The heavens declare the glory of God; the skies proclaim the work of his hands. Day after day they pour forth speech; night after night they reveal knowledge. They have no speech, they use no words; no sound is heard from them. Yet their voice goes out into all the earth, their words to the ends of the world. (Psalm 19:1–4).

Today, will you open your ears and listen for a few minutes? Jesus indicated that Creation will get even louder if he does not receive the praise he deserves. The Pharisees asked Jesus to rebuke the disciples, who were praising him during the triumphal entry into Jerusalem. Jesus responded by saying, "If they keep quiet, the stones will cry out" (Luke 19:40). The rocks are already declaring God's glory, so it's time we joined in the chorus.

Our universe is screaming out that a glorious God is behind it all, but, sadly, most of us have trained ourselves not to listen. Even most Christians are deaf to its testimony.

Now that I know the truth about the stars, I've decided to start my own business to supplement my income. It's called the "Grain of Sand Registry." For only $19.95, you can name a grain of sand after someone you love. I think this is going to be really big! Now, we are not going to send you anything in the mail, but I will personally travel to the Jersey Shore and pick up an individual grain of sand and call it by name, so send your check or money order today!

In all seriousness, our God is amazing. For him, creating a star is no more difficult than creating a speck of sand. So join with creation by declaring God's glory!

Transition Through Reflection...

Weather permitting; take this book outside to finish this chapter. If the weather isn't cooperating today, finish this chapter in front of a window.

Check out some of the things that you typically blow past in your hurried state. Look at the sky, the trees, the grass, and the people. What do these things say about God and his glory?

_____

_____

_____

_____

_____

Read Romans 1:18–25. Why do you think so many people suppress the truth?

_____

_____

_____

_____

_____

It is not that they are ignorant, but that they know the truth and choose to ignore it. Why do we ignore the truth so often?

_____

_____

_____

_____

As you survey God's creation, sing one of the songs below and reflect on God's greatness and majesty.

Suggested Songs

Sing "Indescribable" by Jesse Reeves and Laura Story (popularized by Chris Tomlin). You can also sing "God Of Wonders" by Steve Hindalong and Marc Byrd (popularized by Third Day), "Shout To The Lord" by Darlene Zschech, the hymn "Fairest, Lord Jesus" by August Heinrich von Fallersleben and Joseph August Seiss (New Life Worship has an updated version of this hymn); or the hymn "This Is My Father's World" by Franklin Lawrence Sheppard and Maltbie Davenport Babcock. (Tim Milner has an updated version of this hymn that you can find on iTunes.) (Chord charts are available at www. TransitionsWorship.com).

DAY 6

Multitasking: A Gift Or a Curse?

FOR SOME STRANGE reason, my wife does not seem to appreciate my amazing multitasking skills as much as I do, such as my astonishing ability to watch TV or read a book as I hold a conversation with her. As soon as I feel like I am pretty good at doing two things at once, such as talking to Leah on the phone as I type on my computer at work, I start answering with a generic, "Yes, Honey," but I haven't really listened to her.

The best part of this "skill," which I have developed over 15 years of marriage, is that I am able to repeat her last two sentences at any moment. If she hears the clicking of the computer keys on the other end of the phone and asks me the inevitable question: "Did you hear what I just said?" I have trained my subconscious mind to recall her last statement. Amazing, right?

In all seriousness, if you want to enjoy a long, peaceful marriage, do not attempt to develop this skill. We are so impatient, and we live at such a fast pace, that we tend to divide our attention—often with devastating results.

Some people are better at multitasking than others, but only God can give his full attention to more than one task—or person—at the same time.

I was listening to the news while driving (multitasking) and heard about an iPhone app that turns on your phone's camera while you are texting so you can see what is happening in front of you. The designers insist that they did not intend for this app to be used while driving, only for texting while walking, but texting while driving appears to be the most likely application, in my opinion. You and I would probably agree that this does not seem wise. When it comes to life and death activities, such as highway safety, we realize we need to give them our full attention. But aren't relationships just as important, worthy of your full consideration?

I bet God feels a lot like my wife when I divide my attention between him and all of the other things I think are so important that I cannot set them aside even for a few minutes to worship him. In fact, what is vying for your attention right now as you read this chapter? Stop and write it down so your mind can focus. After all, the point of this book is to draw your attention back to Jesus and to help you remember that he is worthy of your undivided heart.

Do you remember the story of Mary and Martha in Luke 10? You may not realize it, but the story actually has a strong correlation to worship.

As Jesus was passing through Bethany, he and his disciples stopped to visit Mary and Martha. Martha was busy preparing a meal for Jesus and his disciples, which would have been an enormous undertaking. Most likely Martha was cooking for twelve disciples, Jesus, and her brother and sister. Including Martha, the total number of dinner guests was sixteen at minimum. It's quite possible that others were traveling with Jesus as well. In fact, earlier in this chapter, Jesus sent out seventy-two followers to do ministry. Imagine if any of those disciples wanted in on the free meal, since the people who followed Jesus were known for that kind of thing (John 6:26).

Now, think about the difficulty of cooking for a minimum of sixteen people without instant potatoes, Minute Rice, or a microwave. Martha was preparing a huge meal from scratch, and yet the description given of Martha in verse 40 is not "hardworking," "dedicated," or "selfless." Instead, Martha is described as "distracted." What does the use of the word imply?

_____

_____

_____

_____

Martha could have focused her attention on something far superior, as indicated in verse 42b, when Jesus claims, "Mary has chosen what is better..." What could be better than food? Jesus, of course. Mary gave her undivided attention to Jesus, and that was better than what Martha was doing, even though Martha was striving to serve her guests. While it's not wrong to serve, perhaps Martha was doing it out of pride or fear of seeming inadequate rather than a true servant's heart.

No matter what else you are focusing on today, you can never go wrong taking time out for Jesus. If you want to transform your worship, take a few minutes to confess your distracted mind to Jesus and ask him to help you sit at his feet with an undivided heart.

Transition Through Reflection...

Read the full story of Mary and Martha in Luke 10:38–42. What has been distracting you this week?

_____

_____

_____

How do you deal with those distractions?

_____

_____

_____

The answer is not simply to focus harder. In fact, sometimes the very act of trying to focus harder merely builds up the distraction in your mind. Check out what Peter says to do with distractions like worry and anxiety: "Cast all your anxiety on him because he cares for you" (1 Peter 5:7). Give your distractions over to Jesus in prayer so that he can be the only object of your worship.

In Psalm 46:10, the Sons of Korah write from God's perspective, saying, "Be still, and know that I am God; I will be exalted among the nations, I will be exalted in the earth." What are some of the implications of sitting at Jesus' feet in Luke 10:39?

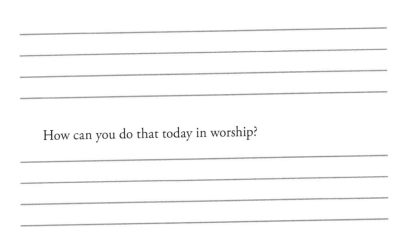

How can you do that today in worship?

Spend some more time listening to Jesus today as he speaks to you through his Word. As a symbol of your desire to maintain an undivided heart, sit on the floor and imagine yourself sitting at the feet of Jesus. Take time to read about Mary's other famous act of worship in John 12:1–8 and Mark 14:1–11.

Suggested Songs

Lemont Hiebert wrote a worship song called "Unashamed Love." The first verse reads, "You call on me to lay aside the worries of my day. To quiet down my busy mind and find a hiding place. Worthy, You are worthy." If you are familiar with this song, sing it in worship right now. If you don't know it, listen to it on YouTube and reflect on the words. You can also sing "We Will Worship You" by Carlos Whittaker and Jason Ingram, "Full Attention" by Jeremy Riddle, or the hymn "Turn Your Eyes Upon Jesus" by Helen H. Lemmel. (Chord charts are available at www. TransitionsWorship.com).

DAY 7

A Styrofoam Blizzard

IRST JOHN 1:9 reads, "If we confess our sins, he is faithful and just and will forgive us our sins and purify us from all unrighteousness." Have you ever wondered why we need to confess our sins to God if he is omniscient? If God knows everything anyway, why must I acknowledge my transgressions? As a pastor, I can probably think of a good theological explanation for the importance of personal confession, but as a father, I have been able to see a glimpse of God's perspective on confession firsthand.

A few years ago when my daughter Jaylea was three-years-old, we spent the day decorating our house for Christmas. Jaylea was playing with the Styrofoam that protected our nativity set, so I asked her to stop. My parenting instincts were a little naïve at the time, because I thought my severe warning was enough to break the stronghold of Styrofoam, which holds sway over every little kid who encounters it.

I left the room for a few minutes, and when I returned, I encountered a Christmas miracle. We had a white Christmas—in the living room. My nativity Styrofoam was broken into little pieces, and some sort of blizzard had apparently blasted white foam all over the room. At least it fit the décor.

"Jaylea, did you do that?" I bellowed.

"No, Daddy, I didn't do it," Jaylea responded as she sat in a pile of Styrofoam. Little white pieces were all over her dress, in her hair, and coming out of her mouth as she denied her involvement.

It took five minutes of showing her the evidence, combined with a host of parental intimidation techniques, before she 'fessed up to the demolition.

I realize this is wishful thinking when dealing with a three-year-old, but imagine if Jaylea had come to me and said, "Daddy, I am so sorry. I disobeyed and played with the Styrofoam. Will you forgive me?" Think of all the grief both of us would have been spared.

Confession is so powerful that it can repair relationships and take them to a much deeper level. In his book *Love Beyond Reason,* John Ortberg says, "The irony is that I hide because I'm afraid that if the full truth about me is known I won't be loved. But whatever is hidden cannot be loved. I can only be loved to the extent that I am known. I can only be fully loved if I am fully known." If you hide who you really are and conceal your sin, you will always wonder if people would love you if they truly knew you. However, I believe that God wants to know you on a personal level, talking with you not just on an omniscient, "I'm God so I know everything" level but as a real person. That's why confession is so important, because it begins a dialogue, which is the foundation of every relationship.

> God knows you fully—every deep, dark secret that you hold inside and don't dare to mutter so much as a whisper—and yet he loves you perfectly.

When I walked into the living room, I knew exactly what Jaylea had done with the Styrofoam. I did not need her to confess in order to know what had happened. Instead, I wanted Jaylea to confess so that she could be restored to unity and be fully loved by her daddy. Like me—and you—Jaylea can only be loved to the extent that she is known. What does your Daddy need to hear from you today?

Transition Through Application...

In John 17:20b–21, Jesus says, "I pray also for those who will believe in me through their message, that all of them may be one, Father, just as you are in me and I am in you." Jesus prayed that we would have the same unity and intimacy with one another as he has with the Father, but it is difficult to be unified with people who we do not really know. Most Christians hide because of the judgmental attitudes of others, so we walk through life with no real unity or intimacy with God's people. Confession builds the intimacy God desires, not only with him but also with each other. James 5:16 says, "Therefore confess your sins to each other and pray for each other so that you may be healed. The prayer of a righteous man is powerful and effective."

Are you willing to take some steps toward unity today with the Father and with his children? Commit yourself to go deeper with your Christian brothers and sisters in the bonds of unity today by choosing a friend or friends with whom you can be accountable. Write down the names of a few friends whom you are willing to approach about accountability.

1. _____

2. _____

3. _____

Allow others to love you more fully as you reveal to them the real you!

Suggested Songs

After you spend some time confessing your secrets to the One who knows you and loves you fully, sing "Lord, I Need You" by Christy Nockels, Daniel Carson, Jesse Reeves, Kristian Stanfill, and Matt Maher (popularized by Chris Tomlin). You can also sing "Search Me, Know Me" by Kathryn Scott and Mildred Rainey or go old school and sing "Refiner's Fire (Purify My Heart)" by Brian Doerksen. If you *really* want to go old school, sing the hymn "I Stand Amazed In The Presence" by Charles Hutchinson Gabriel. (Chord charts are available at www. TransitionsWorship.com).

50 DAYS OF WORSHIP

The Band Goes Into Battle

JEHOSHAPHAT WAS THE sixth king of Judah, and he reigned for twenty-five years. He was a good king who served God in the spirit of David, his forefather. Jehoshaphat certainly made a few mistakes during his reign and faced some difficulties, but for the most part, he followed God wholeheartedly.

At some point during Jehoshaphat's reign, a vast army of Moabites, Ammonites, and Meunites marched out to attack Judah. When Jehoshaphat found out this army was only thirty miles from Jerusalem, he was greatly distressed. He called on all the people of Judah to fast and seek the face of the Lord so that he might deliver them from their enemies. God answered Jehoshaphat and the people through the prophet Jahaziel saying,

> Do not be afraid or discouraged because of this vast army. For the battle is not yours, but God's. Tomorrow march down against them... You will not have to fight

this battle. Take up your positions; stand firm and see the deliverance the LORD will give you, O Judah and Jerusalem. Do not be afraid; do not be discouraged. Go out to face them tomorrow, and the LORD will be with you. (2 Chronicles 20:15–17)

Jehoshaphat seemed to have a fairly powerful army. In fact, 2 Chronicles 17 indicates he had over 1 million troops in Jerusalem who were ready for battle. A reasonable assumption is that the attacking army was either much larger or better equipped than Jehoshaphat's army. Jehoshaphat had made alliances with the northern kingdom of Israel, first with Ahab and then with his sons. Although these alliances were not pleasing to God, Jehoshaphat could have used them to his advantage, trusting in men rather than God. Similarly, he could have abandoned Judah in their time of distress and fled with his family to the northern kingdom. Instead, Jehoshaphat turned to God and asked him to deliver Judah from their enemies. Second Chronicles 20 goes on to report that,

Jehoshaphat bowed down with his face to the ground, and all the people of Judah and Jerusalem fell down in worship before the LORD. Then some Levites from the Kohathites and Korahites stood up and praised the LORD, the God of Israel, with a very loud voice.

Jehoshaphat turned to prayer and worship. This worship service was one of desperation, but certainly not a last resort. He did not exhaust every other avenue of deliverance before turning to God. Prayer and worship were his first and only strategy to preserve his kingdom. Once again, we find the descendants of Korah (see

Day 2: "A Doorman In God's Kingdom") at the center of a crucial worship service. The passage indicates that they praised God with a loud voice.

Speaking of which, don't be that person in your church who complains about the volume of worship. The Lord does not require loud worship, but it is certainly acceptable and pleasing to him. If you feel the volume of worship in your service is unbearable, wear earplugs!

Jehoshaphat set out with many of his people to observe God's deliverance from this great army. In verse 20 he says,

> "Listen to me, Judah and people of Jerusalem! Have faith in the LORD your God and you will be upheld; have faith in his prophets and you will be successful." After consulting the people, Jehoshaphat appointed men to sing to the LORD and to praise him for the splendor of his holiness as they went out at the head of the army, saying: "Give thanks to the LORD, for his love endures forever."

I love this expression of praise, considering the circumstances. Many times, songs of praise are written after God accomplishes something great for his people. For example, Miriam sang the "Song of the Sea" after the Israelites crossed the Red Sea and God delivered them from the Egyptians, and Mary sang the "Magnificat" after the angel Gabriel's visit to announce she would give birth to the Son of God. In a remarkable act of faith, Jehoshaphat sent the praise team out in front of the army. He and the people of Judah marched out to meet their enemies in full faith that God would accomplish what he had promised. If you want to transform your worship, remember that God deserves worship in all circumstances: at church, at work, at home, even on the battlefield.

But Jehoshaphat and his people

sang a song of thanksgiving,

possibly Psalm 136, *before* God

actually fulfilled his promise.

They were so confident that

God would come through that

they praised him in advance of

his deliverance.

Apparently, God was pleased with the worship of his people and chose that particular moment to initiate his rescue plan.

As they began to sing and praise, the LORD set ambushes against the men of Ammon and Moab and Mount Seir who were invading Judah, and they were defeated. The men of Ammon and Moab rose up against the men from Mount Seir to destroy and annihilate them. After they finished slaughtering the men from Seir, they helped to destroy one another." (1 Chronicles 17:22–23)

Transition Through Reflection...

I have heard someone preach on this passage and claim that worship defeated Israel's enemies. Worship is always a response to God, even if it is a response to his promises, but it is not a means of deliverance in and of itself. Worship did not defeat the army; God did. Jehoshaphat and the people of Judah merely trusted God enough to worship him in song and prayer before, during, and after their deliverance.

God has promised to provide for your needs (cf. Philippians 4:19, Matthew 6:25–26). Will you worship God and thank him for his provision even while you are waiting for it to arrive? God has promised to make all things to work together for the good of true disciples of Jesus Christ (Romans 8:28). When you are faced with difficult circumstances, are you willing to worship God and thank him for the relief he will provide even before that relief arrives?

Read the conclusion to the story of Jehoshaphat in 2 Chronicles 20:24–28. The amount of plunder the Israelites took is an indication of the immensity of this invading army. They spent three full days collecting the plunder. Are you facing any difficulties that seem overwhelming? List a few:

1. _____

2. _____

3. _____

4. _____

5. _____

Think back to troubles that have plagued your life in the past and recount the details of how God delivered you from those troubles.

PAST TRIALS	GOD'S DELIVERANCE

If you have neglected to include your redemption from sin, make sure to include that in your list. Since God has been faithful in the past, do you trust him to be faithful in the midst of your current difficulties? Read Isaiah 64:1–5. He might not act within your preferred timeframe, but he will strengthen you as you wait on him in eager expectation of his deliverance.

Suggested Songs

Reflect for a few minutes on the difficulties and needs you have at this time and then join in Jehoshaphat's, the Psalmist's, and Chris Tomlin's words of worship in the song "Forever" and thank God for his future deliverance.

Spend a few extra minutes worshipping Jesus in advance of your liberation with an additional worship song, such as "Everlasting God" by Brenton Brown and Ken Riley (popularized by Chris Tomlin and Lincoln Brewster). You can also sing "Give Thanks" by Henry Smith (popularized by Don Moen); "Your Grace Is Enough" by Matt Maher (popularized by Chris Tomlin); "Your Love Never Fails" by Anthony Skinner and Chris McClarney (popularized by Jesus Culture), focusing on the bridge; or the hymn "The Doxology," by Louis Bourgeois and Thomas Ken. (Gateway Worship has recorded a modern version of this hymn called "The New Doxology.") (Chord charts are available at www.TransitionsWorship.com).

50 DAYS OF WORSHIP

DAY 9

Forgetting To Touch Home

LAST SEASON, I attended a Phillies game and had amazing seats right behind home plate. After the game, I had a three-hour layover before the Eagles game was scheduled to begin. Yes, you read that correctly: Phillies and Eagles in the same day! It was definitely a once in a lifetime opportunity.

My friend from church was at the Phillies game to celebrate his son's seventh birthday. After the game, the birthday boy got to run the bases at Citizen's Bank Park. Since I was hanging out in south Philly for the long haul, I decided to stick around to watch him and about 1,000 other little kids run the bases. You may be thinking, "I'd rather watch grass grow or paint dry," but it was actually pretty interesting.

The area behind the batter's box was roped off so that when the kids reached home plate, they had to turn around and walk back a few feet toward third base to meet their parents and exit the field. What made it so interesting was that many of the kids failed to touch home plate at all. They rounded third and headed toward home, but a few feet before they arrived, they veered off to exit the field.

As I watched, it struck me that roughly ninety-five percent of the boys touched home plate, but only fifty percent of the girls touched it. About half of the girls walked off the field without ever reaching the goal.

In my youth ministry experience, I have had girls who are great ball players and understand that the goal of baseball is to touch home plate. However, it is not farfetched to say that many dads have their sons running (or at least walking) the bases as soon as possible, while many girls are interested in other activities. True to form, that day after the Phillies game, not only did the boys have a better understanding of the goal of baseball, most of them also accomplished that goal with passion. I saw boys stomp on the plate, jump up and land on the plate with two feet, and one little boy even slid into home plate. It exposed a distinct difference between the boys and the girls.

Something similar happens in the Christian life. Some followers of Christ misunderstand their purpose. In Galatians 5:7, Paul says, "You were running a good race. Who cut in on you and kept you from obeying the truth?" Sadly, Paul did not have baseball in his day. Otherwise, he certainly would have used a baseball illustration instead of a dull foot race! Joking aside, Paul is saying that you were rounding third base, and then something or someone caused you to take your eye off the goal and leave the field without touching home plate. For a baseball fan, that is unthinkable! Everything looks like it is going well as you go through the motions of the Christian faith. You show up to church each week, give your tithe, volunteer to help with the children's ministry, and, of course, you sing all the songs. But if you miss the relationship with Jesus in all of that busyness, you are failing to step on home plate.

Don't be discouraged. We're all at different stages in our Christian walk. As we grow in Christ, the goal of the Christian life becomes clearer. For example, I'm sure that if I polled each child who crossed home plate compared to those who didn't, I would find that the kids who crossed were older. Some things just take time to learn.

The Westminster Catechism says, "The chief end and duty of man is to glorify God and enjoy him forever." That sounds like an expression of worship to me. Echoing this sentiment, Isaiah 43:7 says, "The people whom I formed for Myself will declare my praise" (NAS).

We were created to glorify God and enjoy him in a personal relationship. People who understand this point focus their lives around this goal. They take on responsibilities in life with the ultimate goal of fulfilling these purposes. They pursue an education not simply to boost their worldly status and income but to gain a place of influence in the world so they can be a brighter light in the darkness. These people take jobs for the purpose of promoting the gospel of Jesus Christ instead of padding their wallets. They progress in sports so they can coach their community little league team and live as a godly example before unbelievers. Unfortunately, most Christians are not sliding into home with passion. They think that education, the good job, or their amateur sports career is the goal. Rather than a means to an end—sharing the gospel—they make these things ends unto themselves.

> One of the greatest goals we have in this life and the next is to praise God and bring him glory. Our home plate is Jesus. We declare his praise by living a life of worship!

Satan is passionate about one thing in particular: mediocrity. If you are a true follower of Jesus Christ, Satan's ultimate goal isn't to get you to be an unbeliever. His goal is to get you to be an ineffective, unfruitful believer. He wants you to settle for things that seem good but do not help you accomplish the goals God has for your life. Even if your end goal is a 2400 on the SATs, graduating summa cum laude, a Fortune 500 company career, retiring early, or gaining 1,000 friends on Facebook, you are settling for mediocrity and failing to step on home plate, never mind stomp on it or slide into it.

However, we find an incredible truth in Ephesians 5:15–16: "See then that you walk carefully, not as fools, but as wise, redeeming the time, because the days are evil" (KJV 2000). This is the good news: You can redeem the time! That is why I love the baseball analogy, because you get another chance to step up to the plate and run the bases. But this time, don't forget to touch home plate!

Transition Through Reflection...

Read 1 Corinthians 3:10–15. Do you ever wonder why the lives of so many Christians are crumbling around them? We can understand why the lives of non-Christians fall apart, but Christians are supposed to be content in every situation (Philippians 4:12). Why are so many of us unsatisfied and discontent? Because even though we're building on the correct foundation, our building materials are the same wood, hay, and straw that the people of this world use to build. And, just like the three little pigs, your enemy will come along and huff and puff and blow your little house of twigs right over, reducing your Christian life to rubble.

Make a list below of some of your current aspirations and place them on the appropriate side of the list. Are these goals for your glory or God's? Take some time to think about how you can move some of the "straw," the items on the right side of the page, over to the left side. Draw an arrow from the item on the right to the left side of the dividing line to indicate which aspirations you are turning into gold, silver, and costly stones. Finally, make a short note near the arrow indicating how you can transfer those aspirations to God's glory. All of your aspirations can be turned into gold, silver, and costly stones when they are used for God's glory.

ASPIRATIONS	GOD'S GLORY	MY GLORY
GOAL #1		
GOAL #2		
GOAL #3		
GOAL #4		
GOAL #5		
GOAL #6		
GOAL #7		
GOAL #8		

Suggested Songs

Glorify God by singing "Refiner's Fire" (Purify My Heart) by Brian Doerksen. You can also sing "From The Inside Out" by Joel Houston of Hillsong, "In The Secret (I Want To Know You)" by Andy Park, or the hymn "Praise To The Lord The Almighty" by Catherine Winkworth and Joachim Neander. (Chord charts are available at www.TransitionsWorship.com).

DAY 10

Text Message Intimacy

AS I WAS out running errands one day, I heard a story on our local news radio station. It detailed the astonishment of a father who was made aware of his daughter's texting habits when he received the family's cell phone bill. In a single month, this teenager had sent 17,000 texts. When you break that down, she sent an average of two texts per minute throughout the day, including school hours. When you include incoming texts with the outgoing texts, her texts averaged 144 per hour!

I have to admit it: that is an impressive achievement. The news story did not indicate whether the family had unlimited texting, although since the story did not conclude with a homicide investigation, it's probably safe to assume the girl's dad did not have to pay ten cents per text. If her dad can just figure out a way to get her to do her homework and type papers on her phone, it'll be Ivy League all the way.

This story is interesting, because it shows how young people—all of us, really—are desperate for intimacy. The girl in the news story likely used text messaging to fulfill her desire for relationship. However, what should be evident from the number of texts she sent is that no matter how much she communicates with other people, the void in her life will never be filled.

God created us for relationships, but unless we have a relationship with him, all of our other relationships are merely self-serving and will never fill the void in our lives.

Solomon discovered this when he worked his way straight through the list of all the things we think we need to achieve happiness and fulfillment in life. He tried relationships, money, pleasures, fulfilling goals, and intimacy, but nothing worked. Solomon concludes with the following defeatist sentiment: "So I hated life, because the work that is done under the sun was grievous to me. All of it is meaningless, a chasing after the wind" (Ecclesiastes 2:17).

Transition Through Reflection...

What a depressing picture of futility Solomon paints for us! Do you ever chase after the wind? It seems like it's the story of our lives. In fact, it reminds me of when I used to entice my grandma's cat to chase a laser pointer. For all the work the cat put into chasing that light, he would never have anything to show for his efforts. What "shiny lights" are you chasing that you think will fill your desire for intimacy? Take a moment to jot some down.

1. _____

_____

2. _____

_____

3. _____

_____

4. _____

_____

5. _____

_____

6. _____

_____

7. _____

_____

The only shiny thing that will give you meaning, purpose, and hope is the Light Of The World, Jesus Christ (John 8:12). Let us commit to chasing his light, because when we pursue him, he will be found. Proverbs 8:17 says, "I love those who love me, and those who seek me find me."

Read Ecclesiastes 12 to learn about Solomon's answer to the problem of chasing after the wind. Do you trust Solomon's advice? Why or why not?

_____

_____

If so, how has your desire for intimacy been fulfilled by following his advice?

_____

_____

Solomon's ultimate answer is to connect with God, which is implicit in his advice to "remember your Creator" (v. 1), "fear God" (or have reverence for God), and "keep his commandments" (v. 13). Have you connected with God? How have you been chasing him?

Andrew Peterson has a great song called "The Chasing Song" that may help you give more consideration to the worthiness of your earthly pursuits. Find this song on YouTube so you can listen to it right now.

After listening to it, take a few minutes to connect with God by sending him a text message. When you are done, either save it in your "draft" outbox or send it to texttogod.com, a website where other people can see your text (1-559-TXT-2-GOD).[1] The website seems fairly weak on theology, but you can still use it as a symbol of your desire to connect with God. And who knows? Maybe your text will inspire others to connect with God in a deeper way.

Suggested Songs

Declare your commitment to seek "the Light" by lifting your voice and singing "Here I Am To Worship" by Tim Hughes. You can also sing "In The Light" by Charlie Peacock (popularized by DC Talk), "Breathe (Desperate For You)" by Marie Barnett (popularized by Michael W. Smith), the hymn "Turn Your Eyes Upon Jesus" by Helen H. Lemmel, or the hymn "The Light Of The World Is Jesus" By Philip Paul Bliss. (Chord charts are available at www. TransitionsWorship.com).

---

1 I tested this number, and it seems safe, but I cannot guarantee your privacy, so use at your own risk. If you are concerned about the privacy of your cell phone, you can also go to their website and type a message directly. It took about an hour for my text message as well as the message I entered on the website to be posted.

50 DAYS OF WORSHIP

DAY 11

Casting Crowns

GENESIS 1:26 DESCRIBES how God gave humankind dominion over his creation. In light of this, Psalm 8:4–6 explains our place in the universe:

What is man that you are mindful of him, the son of man that you care for him? You made him a little lower than the heavenly beings and crowned him with glory and honor. You made him ruler over the works of your hands; you put everything under his feet.

God has given us authority over all the works of his hands. It seems reasonable that "everything" would include our own lives, yet his desire is that we willingly relinquish control of our lives to him (Luke 9:23, Romans 12:1). Although predestination is a well-supported biblical doctrine, God also gave us the ability to make choices. We can choose to be the lord of our own lives or we can crown him King. He is already the King, but we must humbly recognize this fact and surrender our dominion to his rule. We will not always have this choice. For one day, every living soul who refuses to freely bow the knee to Jesus will be forced to kneel, just as the men who came to arrest Jesus were forced to their knees.

Many people overlook this interesting description of Jesus' arrest in John 18:3–6.

> So Judas came to the grove, guiding a detachment of soldiers and some officials from the chief priests and Pharisees. They were carrying torches, lanterns and weapons. Jesus, knowing all that was going to happen to him, went out and asked them, "Who is it you want?" "Jesus of Nazareth," they replied. "I am he," Jesus said... When Jesus said, "I am he," they drew back and fell to the ground.

The Jewish religious leaders sent a detachment of soldiers, which was normally 600 soldiers, in addition to the officials from the chief priests. We cannot be certain of how many soldiers were there, but it was probably a larger group then we usually imagine. I tend to think of a small unit of ten or twenty soldiers, probably because Mel Gibson wanted to save some money on extras in the garden scene of his movie *The Passion Of The Christ*.

When Jesus identified himself to the mob, every last soldier fell to the ground. What is even more astounding than this display of power is that it had absolutely no effect on the soldiers' hardened hearts. They stood back up and proceeded to arrest Jesus.

The power of Jesus' covenant name, "I Am," forced these hardened soldiers to their knees. It was like a shockwave that gave these men firsthand experience of the power of God.

In a similar way, Paul tells us in Philippians 2:9–11 that, eventually, every knee will bow:

> Therefore God exalted him to the highest place and gave him the name that is above every name, that at the name of Jesus every knee should bow, in heaven and on earth and under the earth, and every tongue confess that Jesus Christ is Lord, to the glory of God the Father.

Will you bow your knee to Jesus in worship today and relinquish control of your life to his rule? Will you cast your crowns at his feet, as in the description of the elders at the throne of God in Revelation 4:10? Before you give an impulsive answer, check out what these "crowns" may actually refer to in Isaiah 62:3: "You will be a crown of splendor in the LORD's hand, a royal diadem in the hand of your God." Ultimately, you are the crown that is thrown at the Lord's feet. It is a picture of ultimate submission to our Lord Jesus Christ—taking off your crown, relinquishing control of your kingdom, and handing it over to Jesus. Lay yourself down at Jesus' feet as you crown him King of your life. Romans 12:1 says, "Therefore, I urge you, brothers, in view of God's mercy, to offer your bodies as living sacrifices, holy and pleasing to God—this is your spiritual act of worship."

If you are knocked to your knees, if you just cannot help but fall down as you are confronted by the greatness of the name of Jesus, please don't harden your heart by paying lip service to God—singing a few songs or saying a few prayers but walking away unchanged by the powerful presence of Jesus. Open your heart to true worship by honoring Jesus in word and deed.

Transition Through Reflection...

Read Luke 9:23–25. What does it mean for you to take up your cross and follow Jesus?

_____

_____

_____

Which areas of your life are you holding back?

_____

_____

Why would God give us dominion in the first place if he desires that we give it back to him?

_____

_____

_____

Do you ever give this kind of freedom to those under your authority (your children, subordinates at work, ministry volunteers) hoping they will ultimately choose to follow your lead? If so, what are the risks in granting such freedom?

_____

_____

_____

What are the benefits?

_____

_____

_____

As you consider those who are under your authority, take time to praise God in your own words for the risk he took in granting you freedom. In all of eternity prior to the creation event, God had never experienced rejection. In giving us freedom, he allowed for the possibility of experiencing rejection for the first time. Will you use your freedom wisely and return it to him as you are motivated by love?

Suggested Songs

Worship Jesus by bowing down before him and singing "We Crown You," by Eddie Kirkland and Steve Fee. You can also sing "We Fall Down" or "Lay Me Down," both by Chris Tomlin; "Build Your Kingdom Here" by Red Collective Experiment; "God & King" (a version of the hymn "All Creatures Of Our God And King") by Zach Neese; or the hymns "Crown him With Many Crowns" by George Job Elvey, Godfrey Thring, and Matthew Bridges and "All Hail The Power" by Edward Perronet, John Rippon, and Oliver Holden. (Chord charts are available at www. TransitionsWorship.com).

DAY 12

Tastykakes And Jesus

DID YOU EVER grab a grocery cart out of the parking lot corral, only to discover it was full of someone else's trash? This is one of my pet peeves. It is not difficult to throw trash in a garbage can, but some people believe their time is so valuable that they use the grocery cart as their own personal trash receptacle instead.

On the positive side, it's interesting to see what people buy in the grocery store and then scarf down before they get to their car. Have you seen these people? They wheel their cart around the store with an open bag of chips sitting in the child seat. The kids have been relegated to the main basket area, and everyone is munching away. They fully intend to pay for their snacks when they get to the register, but it is certainly not going to be a full bag at that point.

One evening as I visited our local grocery store, I grabbed a cart from the corral and was pleasantly surprised to find a Tastykakes box in the basket. For those of you outside the Philadelphia area, Tastykakes are similar to a Hostess type snack, only better. As I reached down to pick up the box, I thought surely there must be a few Tastykakes left, because how could anyone eat an entire box of Tastykakes by the time they reached the parking lot? Clearly someone had simply overlooked the box as they were packing groceries into their car, and their loss was about to be my gain. (Of course, as a godly man I fully intended to return the box of Tastykakes to the grocery store's lost and found, hoping to collect the reward that I am certain the rightful owners would extend to me as a token of their appreciation!)

Mouth watering, I reached out to inspect the box and was overcome with disappointment. Apparently, this Tastykake connoisseur was pretty psyched about his or her curbside snack, because the box had been ripped open, and not a crumb was left. Whoever it was must have had some appetite, but I'm afraid it is a craving that is difficult to satisfy, because the way sugar and fat work, they provide you with only a brief high, and before long, you're hungry for more.

I think this is how some people approach Jesus. They are so hungry for more than this life has to offer that when they get a taste of the eternal, they jump right in and eat it up. They tear open God's Word and devour it. But once the initial good feelings fade, they discard it and move on to something else that will give them a new high. Jesus spoke about this in Matthew 13 in the Parable of the Sower. Read verses 1–23. The person who receives the seed that fell on the rocky soil receives the gospel joyfully. Sadly, it does not last, because his roots are shallow, so when he is faced with persecution, he falls away. Verse 22 goes on to say, "The seed falling among the thorns refers to someone who hears the word, but the worries of this life and the deceitfulness of wealth choke the word, making it unfruitful."

Many of us are only interested in the emotional high that we get upon initially hearing about Jesus' love, attending church, and singing his praises. Our faith must be based on a relationship with Jesus Christ. Just like any relationship, there will be highs and lows. If you persevere in Christ, at times your relationship will feel stagnant and as empty as that Tastykakes box. Do not give up, because during such times we are called to live by faith knowing he is the only one who truly satisfies. The plant that sprang up from the seed sown among the thorns grew quickly and seemed healthy at first, but those who received it were searching for a quick fix experience rather than a relationship. They hurried on to wealth, entertainment, and worldly interests to get their next "sugar high."

But our faith should not be about chasing one emotional high after another.

Hebrews 13:5 says, "Keep your lives free from the love of money and be content with what you have, because God has said, 'Never will I leave you; never will I forsake you.'" Jesus also said in John 4:14, "but whoever drinks the water I give them will never thirst. Indeed, the water I give them will become in them a spring of water welling up to eternal life." God's presence is the only thing that really satisfies—even and *especially* when you don't feel like that's true.

Transition Through Reflection...

Read Isaiah 55. Make a list of some of the cares of this world that have been tugging at your heart, tempting you to find your satisfaction apart from Christ.

1. _____

2. _____

3. _____

4. _____

_____

5. _____

_____

God says his Word will accomplish what he desires. What do you believe God is trying to accomplish in your life through Isaiah 55 and the other scriptures you read today?

_____

_____

As we submit to God's commands and seek his will, we will be filled with joy and peace (v. 12). Commit to meditating on this truth throughout your day: "Blessed are those who hunger and thirst for righteousness, for they will be filled" (Matthew 5:6). If you are willing, write this verse on your hand and read it every time you notice it today. And if someone else notices it and asks about it, share the gist of this devotion with them!

Suggested Songs

Sing "Christ Is Enough" by Hillsong and run to Jesus even if your feelings conflict with what you know in faith to be true. You can also sing "Enough" by Chris Tomlin and Louie Giglio, "Seek Ye First," by Karen Lafferty, "Hungry (Falling On My Knees)" by Kathryn Scott, "You Are My All In All" by Dennis Jernigan, or "As The Deer" by Martin Nystrom. (Chord charts are available at www. TransitionsWorship.com).

50 DAYS OF WORSHIP

DAY 13

Smaller And Lesser

THE GAME "BIGGER Or Better" is a popular team-building activity amongst youth groups. It's similar to a scavenger hunt, but instead of finding predetermined items, team members must trade an item, like a pencil or a plastic fork, for something bigger or better. When the time limit has expired, they return to the central location to determine which team was able to trade up to the most valuable commodity.

This game has been around for a long time. It was made popular by a Canadian named Kyle MacDonald. Starting with a red paperclip, over the course of a year, Kyle made fourteen different trades. He traded the paperclip for a pen and eventually bartered up to a collector's snow globe. He traded the snow globe for a speaking role in one of Corben Bernsen's upcoming movies. Finally, Kyle exchanged the movie job for a house!

While there is nothing wrong with playing a team-building game like this; unfortunately, this is the philosophy under which most people in our world operate. Dissatisfied with what God has provided for us, we take matters into our own hands and try to upgrade to what we consider to be bigger and better. The pattern of this world is to equate being happy with getting more and more stuff, but God's philosophy is diametrically opposed to this way of thinking. Rather than get more, to be truly content, we must be willing to *give up* more and more to Christ's control. Jesus has already given us everything we need to live a contented life. Ephesians 1:3 says, "Praise be to the God and Father of our Lord Jesus Christ, who has blessed us in the heavenly realms with every spiritual blessing in Christ." We already have every spiritual blessing we need to live life to the full. In fact, 2 Peter 1:3 says, "His divine power has given us everything we need for a godly life through our knowledge of him who called us by his own glory and goodness."

> As believers, if we are not content, it is not because we lack anything, it is probably because we have too much.

At times, I am absolutely guilty of thinking, "How can this be true? I could use a lot more from God." If you can relate, then understand we are both missing Jesus' counter-cultural secret to achieving a life of contentment. He has already given us everything! If you feel like you are missing something, it is probably because you are holding on too tightly to things you need to turn over to him.

John the Baptist understood this better than most Christians throughout history. John had a very popular ministry, so popular that Matthew says, "People went out to him from Jerusalem and all Judea and the whole region of the Jordan" (Matthew 3:5). However, not long after John started drawing crowds, Jesus began his public ministry. As people flocked to Jesus, a few of John's disciples became jealous. They came to John and reported, "Rabbi, that man who was with you on the other side of the Jordan—the one you testified about—look, he is baptizing, and everyone is going to him." If you want to know what worship really looks like, listen to John's response: "[Jesus] must become greater, and I must become less" (John 3:30). We need more worshippers like John the Baptist! Martin Luther said, "God creates out of nothing. Therefore, until a man is nothing, God can make nothing out of him." Are you willing to become nothing, leaving your ego at the door as you worship Jesus, or does the "bigger and better" philosophy have a hold of your heart?

My former youth groups attended a Christian music festival called Creation each summer. Usually, we had teenagers visit our campsite throughout the week in the midst of playing "Bigger and Better." Such a large number of teens came begging for our supplies that many members of our group began to detest the game. After a few years of this, we decided to print our own T-shirts with the slogan, "Jesus hates bigger and better, and so do we. Smaller and lesser, that's Jesus' motto."

If you're completely honest, what is the motto of your current lifestyle—bigger and better or smaller and lesser?

Transition through Application...

Read the remainder of John the Baptist's philosophy of worship in John 3:22–36. John said that he is the best man, and Jesus is the groom. What is the best man's job? To attend to the needs of the groom, to support him, and to make the groom look good. The best man does not take the spotlight on the wedding day. Instead, he reflects the spotlight onto the groom.

The same is true for the ladies. The whole purpose of bridesmaids is to make the bride look good. Have you ever wondered why some bridesmaids hate their dresses? They get stuck with hideous dresses, because their job is to stand there and look ugly so that the bride stands out as radiant and beautiful. That might be a bit of an exaggeration, but you get the point. Bridesmaids are more like the leaves that compliment and direct our attention to the rose. This is what John the Baptist did for Jesus. "He must become greater; I must become less." If you really want to transform your worship, shine the light on Jesus and promote his fame instead of yours.

What is one way that Jesus can become greater in your life today and you can become less?

_____

_____

_____

_____

_____

Serving others anonymously is a fantastic way to shine the light on Jesus while diminishing your own ego. Do something nice for a friend or neighbor and then leave a note saying, "Jesus loves you" or quote James 1:17, "Every good and perfect gift is from above."

Suggested Songs

Ask God to change your mindset from "bigger and better" to "smaller and lesser" today as you sing Chris Tomlin's version of the hymn "When I Survey The Wondrous Cross" called "The Wonderful Cross" (co-authored by J.D. Walt, Jesse Reeves, and Lowell Mason). You can also sing "You" by Joel Houston of Hillsong; "Lead Me To The Cross" by Brooke Ligertwood (popularized by Chris & Conrad); "Empty Me" by Gene Way and John Comer (popularized by Jeremy Camp); "Shout Your Fame" by Gio Galanti, Jonas Myrin, Natasha Bedingfield, and Paul Nevison of Hillsong; or the hymn "Be Thou My Vision" by Eleanor Henrietta Hull and Mary Elizabeth Byrne. (Chord charts are available at www. TransitionsWorship.com).

DAY 14

Giving or Getting?

WHILE I WAS sitting at the kitchen table performing super glue surgery on my son Gibson's Star Wars spaceship, he approached me and asked, "Dad, can I have candy?" Gibson, who was six years old at the time, is our candy-a-holic. He loves candy and would consume it all day if left to his own devices. He had already enjoyed his one candy for the day, so I said, "No candy."

"Dad, *please* can I have candy?"

"No, Gibson."

"Can I just have a really small piece?"

"No!"

Gibson paused for a minute and then regrouped. "Dad, *do you mind* if I have a candy?"

"No!"

"Thanks, Dad!" Gibson said with a devious smirk.

Unbelievable! At age six, this kid was already scamming me.

Gibson's trick made me think about my own motivations when it comes to serving my Heavenly Father. How many times are my motivations all about manipulating God to get what I want? James 4:2–3 says, "You do not have, because you do not ask God. When you ask, you do not receive, because you ask with wrong motives, that you may spend what you get on your pleasures." In light of this, ask yourself the following question: Why do you attend a church service?

_____

_____

_____

_____

Most Christians will darken the doorways of local assemblies every Easter Sunday, and yet, sadly, attendance is down ten to twenty percent the following Sunday. I learned of two churches that employed all kinds of tactics to entice people to attend on Easter. One church held a Jonas Brothers concert to get people in the door. Another mega church in Texas offered $4 million in prizes. Yeah, you heard that correctly. They gave away two BMWs, an Audi, a Mitsubishi Eclipse, a Jaguar, and all kinds of other items. You're probably thinking, "That's horrible! Jesus would have flipped over the tables in that place." But if you are completely honest, you will probably admit to thinking, "I wish I had known about that church prior to Easter!"

Think about the question above again: Why do you attend a church service? Do you attend so you can be entertained? Do you go to the service just to feel good about yourself? Do you worship God for what you

> Worship is the complete submission of our complete selves, our total response to God in faith. Selfishness and submission cannot coexist.

can get out of him or because you are grateful for what he has already given you? He has given you so much more than a BMW. He has given you new life.

Transition Through Reflection...

Read the account in John 6:23–29 of what happens after Jesus fed the 5,000. Why did the people follow Jesus to the other side of the Sea of Galilee?

_____

_____

Is it at all likely that they knew their motivations were wrong? Usually, we assume that our motivations are pure, because we evaluate ourselves with a different standard than we evaluate others. If you really want to transform your worship, be honest and evaluate your motivations for worshiping Jesus, going to church, studying the Word, or even reading this book. Are you just skimming through it to mark it off your checklist, or are you spending time on the worship activities?

If you struggle to truly know your own heart, pray as David prayed in Psalm 139:23–24, "Search me, O God, and know my heart; test me and know my anxious thoughts. See if there is any offensive way in me...." Take some time today to speak with God and ask him to give you an undivided heart that is devoted to him above all else (Psalm 86:11).

Suggested Songs

If you're willing to make a commitment to focus on Jesus instead of yourself, verbalize this promise by singing "Jesus, Lover Of My Soul (It's All About You)" by Paul Oakley (popularized by Passion). You can also sing "You Are God Alone," by Billy J. Foote and Cindy Foote (popularized by Philips, Craig, and Dean), "In Christ Alone" by Keith Getty and Stuart Townend; or the hymn "Crown him with Many Crowns" by George Job Elvey, Godfrey Thring, and Matthew Bridges. Finally, listen to the song "Search Me" by The Bridge Band. As you worship, say to Jesus, "I am here for your glory, not mine. Please help me to put your interests above mine, truly making you the Lord of my life and worshipping you the way you deserve to be worshipped." (Chord charts are available at www.TransitionsWorship.com).

50 DAYS OF WORSHIP

Michael Jackson Kind Of Worship

THREE WEEKS BEFORE Michael Jackson died, a famous Christian singer named Andrae Crouch and his sister Sandra went to visit him at his recording studio. Andrae recorded about twenty albums throughout the 1970s, 80s, and 90s. He was also a friend of Michael's and had even produced some of his songs.

During their time with Michael, Andrae and Sandra had a chance to talk to him about Jesus and the topic of worship. Describing that experience, Andrae's spokesperson said,

Andrae and Sandra did in fact visit with Michael Jackson two times, once at the recording studio and once at his home in the last two months, as recently as three weeks ago, asking for prayer concerning... how he could make his music more "spiritual" ... he wanted to know what makes your hands go up, and makes you "come out of yourself," and what gives a "spirituality" to the music? Then he requested to hear his favorite song that he loves and wanted them to sing to him, so they... joined hands and sang together, and he said, "It was beautiful." ... He definitely had an encounter with them.

Sadly, in another press release, Sandra made it clear that although Michael may have had an encounter with her and her brother, he did not encounter the risen and reigning Lord Jesus Christ that day.

Did you notice what Michael was searching for? He was longing for an *experience*. He wanted to put his hands up in worship and feel excited. He wanted to get an ecstatic sensation as he sang his music.

Pause for a moment to let that sink in. The primary objective of worship is not to generate a good feeling. Good feelings are merely a byproduct. Instead, worship is our total response to God in faith. You might not get any warm fuzzies after following through with the activities in this book, and that is okay, because worship is not primarily about your feelings. In fact, worship is not directed toward you at all.

Like Michael, too many people worship experiences rather than God.

The Bible is clear that worship should take place no matter how we feel. In Leviticus 10, when Aaron's sons Nadab and Abihu rebelled against God's commands, God consumed them with fire. Moses instructed Aaron and his two remaining sons, who were Israel's priests, that they were not permitted to mourn in the traditional way for Nadab and Abihu. In verse 6, Moses gives these instructions: "Do not let your hair become unkempt and do not tear your clothes, or you will die... But your relatives, all the Israelites, may mourn for those the

Lord has destroyed by fire." How could God be so cold and heartless to require that these men not mourn outwardly for their loved ones?

We must remember that God was completely just in taking the lives of Nadab and Abihu, and even in the midst of suffering, he is still worthy of worship. Since Aaron and his two remaining sons were the representatives for the Israelites, it was necessary for them to continue their priestly duties no matter how they felt. God's people, including priests, are supposed to enter his presence with a joyful noise no matter the circumstances of life (cf. Psalm 95:2, 100:1, Philippians 4:4).

The robe that Aaron wore as part of his priestly garments had gold bells sown into the hem, apparently to symbolize continual praise in God's presence (Exodus 28:33–35). God deserves continual praise from us believers as well. Philippians 4:4 says, "Rejoice in the Lord always. I will say it again: Rejoice!"

If you really want to transform your worship, your mood swings and the circumstances of your life should have no bearing on the worship God receives. In his book *In a Pit With a Lion on a Snowy Day,* Mark Batterson says it like this, "Don't let what's wrong with you keep you from worshiping what's right with God." Feelings and experiences are of secondary importance to responding to God in faith—and by that I mean a distant second!

Don't make the same mistake Michael Jackson made by seeking experiences instead of God. God is worthy of your worship today whether you get the warm fuzzies or not.

Transition Through Reflection...

Read 2 Peter 1:16–21. Peter had many amazing experiences. He walked on water with Jesus (at least for a couple of seconds), he witnessed Jesus multiply the fish and the loaves, he stood by when Jesus raised Lazarus from the dead, performed miracles, and, of course, was an eyewitness to the transfiguration of Jesus. (The transfiguration is actually what Peter was referring to in verses 17–18.) Peter's experiences were well beyond what we can imagine, and yet Peter goes on in verse 19 to tell us what is more important than all of these experiences. The King James Version of the Bible expresses Peter's point very clearly: "We have also a more sure word of prophecy." To what word of prophecy is he referring? Reread verse 20 if you are not sure before continuing on to the answer.

_____

_____

Peter is referring to the Scriptures. The Scriptures are "more sure" than what?

_____

_____

They are more sure than what Peter was just referencing—his experience of the transfiguration of Jesus. If the Scriptures trump Peter's amazing experiences, it also trumps yours. In light of that, will you focus on your experience in worship or God's truth? God's truth says we are capable of and required to "Rejoice in the Lord always. I will say it again: Rejoice!"

Suggested Songs

I hope you will focus on God's truth today instead of your experience in worship as you sing "10,000 Reasons (Bless The Lord)" by Jonas Myrin and Matt Redman. You can also sing, "Blessed Be Your Name" by Beth Redman and Matt Redman, "Jesus, Lover of My Soul (It's All About You)" by Paul Oakley (popularized by Passion), or the hymn "To God Be The Glory" by Fanny Jane Crosby and William Howard Doane. (Chord charts are available at www. TransitionsWorship.com).

DAY 16

The Lethal Lollipop

HAVE YOU EVER discovered that something you thought was really good for you is actually bad for you instead? At Christmas time, the secretary at my church had a giant lollipop tree on her desk in the main office, so one day I helped myself to a treat. But on my first lick, I cut my tongue on a sharp edge. It was like a lollipop razor blade. My tongue was literally bleeding. What are the chances of something like that happening? I thought this lollipop was going to be to my profit. Instead, it hurt me, causing me pain and loss.

Paul talks about this principle in Philippians 3:7–9, albeit a little more seriously than my lollipop mishap.

> But whatever was to my profit I now consider loss for the sake of Christ. What is more, I consider everything a loss compared to the surpassing greatness of knowing Christ Jesus my Lord, for whose sake I have lost all

things. I consider them rubbish, that I may gain Christ and be found in him, not having a righteousness of my own that comes from the law, but that which is through faith in Christ—the righteousness that comes from God and is by faith.

Everything Paul accomplished and achieved in his own strength and for his own glory he calls garbage. Why? These were the very things that caused him to rely on himself rather than God.

The things Paul thought were a source of profit were the very things that were killing him.

Can you think of anything in your life that you thought was profitable but actually caused you to take your eyes off Christ? For me, money often has this effect. I want more and more of it, but when I get it, it causes me to focus on things rather than Christ. All of us have distractions that seem good but, upon further reflection, draw us away from Christ. Maybe it is elevating education to an obsessive place in your life so you skip Bible studies and church services to study more. Or maybe it's your job. It seemed very profitable at first, but it keeps you from serving others and fulfilling the purpose for which God created you. Maybe it's the friendship you developed with a co-worker of the opposite sex that started out as a profitable relationship but has since become a detriment to your marriage. What other things in your life seemed good at first but are now drawing you away from God and sucking up all of your time and energy?

I heard a story once about how Eskimos hunt wolves. They take a sharp knife, dip it in blood, and then freeze it. They do this multiple times so that a thick layer of blood conceals the blade. Then they secure the handle in the ground so that only the blood-covered blade is exposed.

When the wolf comes along, he smells the blood and starts to lick the frozen blood. The blood tastes so good that he licks faster and harder until the blade of the knife is exposed. The wolf is so overwhelmed by his insatiable desire for blood that he doesn't even notice when the taste of frozen blood is replaced by the warm blood from his own tongue. The wolf will continue to lick the blade until he dies from blood loss.

In the same way, Satan will often give us sharp lollipops that look really good at first glance but end up destroying us spiritually. As for me, I'm just glad I was smart enough to set the lollipop aside after one lick!

Transition through Application...

To prepare yourself for worship, take a few minutes to pray and ask God to reveal examples of things you thought were to your profit but are actually considered a loss from the point of view of God's kingdom. Grab a separate piece of paper and make a list of those lethal "lollipops" in your life. These may not necessarily be obvious sins, just things that seem to be productive and beneficial on the surface but are really consuming time and energy that could be used to serve God. This may take a few additional moments of prayer and reflection. Ask God to give you Paul's attitude toward these lethal lollipops, then crumple up your paper and throw it in the garbage to express your acknowledgement that these things are "rubbish." If you want to take this to the next level, and if it's possible to do so, physically throw away any of the items on your list.

Suggested Songs

Sing "Lead Me To The Cross" by Brooke Ligertwood (popularized by Chris and Conrad). The words of the pre-chorus are: "Everything I once held dear, I count it all as loss." If you can think of anything in your life that is a detriment to your relationship with God, commit to discarding it as garbage and then sing this song as a prayer of commitment. You can also sing "Knowing You" by Graham Kendrick (popularized by Robin Mark), "Surrender" by Marc James, or Chris Tomlin's version of the hymn "Wondrous Cross." (Chord charts are available at www.TransitionsWorship.com).

50 DAYS OF WORSHIP

DAY 17

I Don't Think God Will Mind

A FEW YEARS AGO, Catholic cardinals and bishops around the United States made an exception from the normal tradition of abstaining from meat on Friday during Lent. That year, the second Friday of Lent happened to fall on St. Patrick's Day, so the leaders of the Catholic Church told their followers they were free to eat meat that day. I'm not Catholic, so if the leaders of that church want to suspend their traditions when they determine it is appropriate, that's fine with me. After all, Lent is not a biblical tradition; it's a church tradition. As long as a tradition does not violate biblical principles, people should practice their traditions in whatever way they see fit.

However, I did take exception to the commentary of a reporter on my local radio station who said, "I don't think God will mind." Those are dangerous words. I realize I implied the same thing in what I wrote above, because Lent is a human tradition and not a biblical command, but it was the attitude with which the reporter made the statement that felt dangerous.

I'll bet many people have uttered similar words throughout history. For example, I'm sure Korah (see "Day 2: A Doorman In God's Kingdom") said something along those lines when he tried to take the priesthood from Aaron. I suppose Nadab and Abihu (see "Day 15: Michael Jackson Kind of Worship") said something like that when they lit their own fire on God's altar. And I am fairly certain Uzzah (see "Day 1: Sincerity Versus Obedience") probably thought something similar when he reached out his hand to steady the Ark.

Is your Christianity filled with justifications like this? Do you find yourself thinking or saying, "I don't think God will mind"?

> God's Word draws a line in the sand, and we try to get our toes as close to the edge as possible, all the while touting our slogan, "I don't think God will mind."

Why do we keep doing this? The people of Isaiah's day did the same thing. Isaiah 1:11–13 says,

"The multitude of your sacrifices—what are they to me?" says the Lord. "I have more than enough of burnt offerings, of rams and the fat of fattened animals; I have no pleasure in the blood of bulls and lambs and goats. When you come to appear before me, who has asked this of you, this trampling of my courts? Stop bringing meaningless offerings!"

The people thought they could become ceremonially clean before God by offering sacrifices, often multiple sacrifices. They thought to themselves, "Oh, I've been extra bad this week, but that's okay.

I'll just offer two extra sacrifices. That should cover it." But multiple sacrifices and heaping up prayers are meaningless to God and do not please him when we refuse to bring our lives into conformity with his standards. The prophet Samuel made this clear when he said to King Saul, "Does the LORD delight in burnt offerings and sacrifices as much as in obeying the voice of the LORD? To obey is better than sacrifice, and to heed is better than the fat of rams" (1 Samuel 15:22).

This is where Lent can become displeasing to God. How can those who observe this tradition think God is pleased after they get drunk and party all night on St. Patty's Day and then give up meat the next week to cover their guilt? Even embracing a fanatical vegan lifestyle from now until death will not cover a single sin. Hebrews 11:6 says, "And without faith it is impossible to please God, because anyone who comes to him must believe that he exists and that he rewards those who earnestly seek him."

We need to reject the "I don't think God will mind" slogan and worship God the way he wants to be worshipped. God requires faith in the death and resurrection of his Son Jesus Christ as the atonement for our sins. If you are living in opposition to God, then attending a few church services and singing a couple of worship songs will not please him. In fact he will answer you like he did the people of Isaiah's day: "Stop bringing meaningless offerings!"

Transition Through Application...

You may have noticed that I have used this theme several times throughout this book. I believe that understanding this concept is essential to worshipping God in a way that pleases him. Worship is not just standing around singing some songs; it is our total response to God in faith, including a life lived in obedience to him. Jesus said,

"If you love me, keep my commands" (John 14:15). Even if you are a committed, evangelical Christian, have you been subtly trying to cover your sin by giving God your religious traditions?

Repentance is the only acceptable response to our acknowledgement of sin. Instead of looking at worshipping God through obedience as a theoretical idea that you need to abide by at some other time when you are living "normal life," read the following Scriptural commands and then put them into practice. Will you commit to worshipping Jesus by obeying one of these commands each day this week?

DAY 1: Read 1 Thessalonians 4:13–18 and Hebrews 10:24–25. Paul instructs us to "encourage one another with these words." Will you worship God through obedience by calling or e-mailing a Christian brother or sister to encourage him or her with the truth that Jesus is returning? How about a foreign missionary from your church? Let the person know he or she is not forgotten and that the work the person is doing is vitally important as Jesus' return draws near.

DAY 2: Read Matthew 5:23–24. I like how Jesus phrases this command. We assume that only someone who feels like he or she has been wronged is required to initiate restoration. When we hear that a person is angry with us, sometimes we are tempted to think, "Well, they need to do the right thing and come to me if they are upset so we can talk about it." We tend to put the obligation on the shoulders of the offended, but Jesus indicates that even if you hear that someone is angry with you, you should initiate contact and be reconciled. Will you worship God through obedience by contacting someone right now who you know is angry with you?

DAY 3: Read 1 Thessalonians 5:11. Do you know a brother or sister who is hurting? Will you worship God through obedience by searching for a card around your house right now and writing that person a comforting note?

DAY 4: Read Matthew 28:19. This may be a tough one for you, but remember, obedience to this command is the kind of worship God desires. Will you worship God through obedience by sharing the gospel with someone right now? I realize you may be sitting at home reading this book and may not have access to someone who needs to hear the gospel. If so, consider writing an e-mail to a loved one and letting the person know God has placed him or her on your heart. Share how much God loves that person.

DAY 5: Read 1 Thessalonians 5:12–15. Paul shares a number of instructions here. Will you worship God through obedience by choosing one of the actions in 1 Thessalonians 5 to follow through with right now?

Suggested Songs

As you sing "Give Me Faith" by Elevation Worship, commit to giving God a living faith as evidenced by obedience. You can also sing "Lay Me Down" by Chris Tomlin, "Lord, Reign In Me" by Brenton Brown, "Take My Life (Holiness)" by Scott Underwood, or the hymn "Take My Life And Let It Be" by Frances Ridley Havergal and Henri Abraham Cesar Malan. (Chord charts are available at www. TransitionsWorship.com).

DAY 18

The Debt

EVEN THOUGH WE have a Wii, my kids must be video game deprived, because whenever my friends come over to visit, they beg to play games on my friends' iPhones or iPads. At ages six and three, my daughters, Jaylea and Trinity, downloaded some free apps on my friend's phone. They wanted to play games like "Dream Dresses," "My Horse," and "Tap Pet Hotel." My friend tells me he is still slightly embarrassed when an advertisement for Dream Dresses pops up on his phone while he's in a meeting.

Recently, however, he was more than embarrassed. He came over and showed me his iTunes bill. Apparently, my daughters downloaded $28.83 of in-app purchases on his account. The girls purchased 450 Gems from My Horse for $19.99, stacks of gems and treats from Tap Pet Hotel for $3.98, and a few other things.

Now, $28.83 probably doesn't seem like a big deal to you, but the size of a debt is relative to the income of the debtor. Needless to say, this is a substantial sum for two little girls like my daughters. In fact, there is no possible way for Jaylea and Trinity to pay it, because they have no income. They don't even get an allowance yet. They have no credit cards and no way to negotiate with iTunes. They need a mediator to handle this situation and a redeemer to pay their debt. So who do you think is going to redeem that bill? That's right, their father.

You and I have also incurred a debt that we cannot possibly repay. Our debt is sin. Jesus calls sin a debt in Matthew 6:12. He taught us to ask God to "forgive us our debt." Jesus shares a parable in Matthew 18 to help us understand the significance of our debt.

> We tend to underestimate the debt we have incurred.
>
> Remember, the size of a debt is relative to the income of the debtor.

Therefore, the kingdom of heaven is like a king who wanted to settle accounts with his servants. As he began the settlement, a man who owed him ten thousand talents was brought to him. Since he was not able to pay, the master ordered that he and his wife and his children and all that he had be sold to repay the debt. The servant fell on his knees before him. "Be patient with me," he begged, "and I will pay back everything." The servant's master took pity on him, canceled the debt and let him go. (Matthew 18: 23–27)

The word *talent* does not mean much to us today, so we need to understand it in its original context. When Jesus shared this story, a talent was their largest monetary unit. Today, our largest bill in the United States is the $100 bill. However, in our history, there have been $500, $1,000, $5,000, and even $10,000 bills. In fact, in 1934, a $100,000 bill was created, although it was not circulated amongst the general public.

Now that we understand that a talent was the most valuable denomination of money in the first century, the next detail to consider is that 10,000 was the largest numerical term in the ancient Greek language. They did not have a word for anything larger than 10,000. Therefore, Jesus is making the point that this man owed the largest possible debt. In fact, Herod the Great was in charge of all the territories around Israel—including Judea, Samaria, and Galilee—and the yearly taxes he collected from all of his people totaled only 900 talents. That means this servant owed about eleven years' worth of taxes from an entire country. His debt was beyond imagination!

Jesus told this story, because he wanted us to understand that our sin debt is impossible to repay on our own. We have trouble understanding the enormity of our debt, because it is also beyond our comprehension. We tend to look at sin in the context of big sins and little sins, but Scripture teaches that every sin is an attack on the nature of God. After David committed adultery and murder, he admitted to God, "Against You, You only, have I sinned" (Psalm 51:4). Because all sin is ultimately directed at God, who is eternal, sin requires an eternal punishment that will cost us everything we have, including our very lives. As Romans 6:23 says, "The wages of sin is death."

This is not a debt you can pay on your own or that someone else can pay for you. Psalm 49:7–8 says, "No man can redeem the life of another or give to God a ransom for him—the ransom for a life is costly, no payment is ever enough." Like my daughters, you and I need a mediator to intercede on our behalf and bring about a resolution. A mediator needs to represent both parties involved in the dispute, so in order to represent both God and man, God the Son became a man. I

Timothy 2:5–6 says, "For there is one God and one mediator between God and men, the man Christ Jesus, who gave himself as a ransom for all men." Jesus became our redeemer and paid the ransom for our sin debt. He paid the highest price imaginable to redeem you and me.

> For you know that it was not with perishable things such as silver or gold that you were redeemed from the empty way of life handed down to you from your forefathers, but with the precious blood of Christ, a lamb without blemish or defect. (1 Peter 1:18–19)

Because Jesus paid this debt, we now belong to him. First Corinthians 6:20 says, "You were bought at a price. Therefore honor God with your body."

In Jesus' parable, the servant who was forgiven this enormous debt turned around and demanded payment from a fellow servant who owed him 100 denarii. One denarius equaled about one day's wages. It is evident that the forgiven servant did not appreciate the cost of his deliverance. His debt did not just vanish; the master absorbed it, just as Jesus absorbed our sin debt on the cross. Do you understand and appreciate the cost of your deliverance? If you refuse to forgive the relatively small debts of others, you do not understand Jesus' sacrifice for you.

In the parable, the master turns the unforgiving servant over to the jailers to be tortured until his full debt was paid. Jesus concludes with this chilling statement, "This is how my heavenly Father will treat each of you unless you forgive your brother from your heart" (v. 35). If you appreciate the deliverance from your debt, then honor God by forgiving your debtors and by praising Jesus for paying your ransom.

Transition Through Application...

In the previous devotional ("I Don't Think God Will Mind"), I encouraged you to reconcile with someone who was offended by your actions. In light of what you just read, take the opportunity to honor Jesus' sacrifice by forgiving a debt that is owed to you. Has someone offended you or sinned against you, and you know you have been holding onto your rights, unwilling to forgive? You probably assume that I am going to say, "Just forgive them and move on." Actually, what I would like you to do is rebuke them! Are you starting to like this book even more?

Hold on a second! You need to understand this, so let me see if I can clear up what you're supposed to do. If someone has offended you, but it does not qualify as a "sin" issue, then I encourage you to either share your hurt with that person or overlook the offense. Proverbs 19:11 says, "It is to one's glory to overlook an offense." However, if someone has sinned against you, you are not told to simply forgive and forget. It's actually more difficult than that. Check out Luke 17:3–4, "If your brother or sister sins against you, rebuke them; and if they repent, forgive them. Even if they sin against you seven times in a day and seven times come back to you saying 'I repent,' you must forgive them."

On his blog, Gary Thomas, author of *Sacred Marriage* says, "You have no right to pronounce pardon when the Holy Spirit wants to bring conviction." If someone has sinned against you, you need to make him or her aware of the transgression. If the person repents, you should forgive him or her. If the person refuses to acknowledge the sin, you should appeal to a mediator who is willing to join you in bringing a rebuke against the offender, according to Matthew 18. This must be done with a broken heart and a desire to reconcile, understanding that Jesus has been exceedingly patient with you.

Are you willing to honor God by taking the difficult step of contacting the person or people who have sinned against you? If so, write down the name of someone who has sinned against you:

_____

_____

This act of obedience is a component of your total response to God in faith and will help facilitate your transition from singer to worshipper. Read Matthew 18:15–17 for more direction on how to handle conflicts with your brothers and sisters in Christ.

Suggested Songs

Worship Jesus by singing an old song that captures this concept well: "He Paid A Debt" by Ellis J. Crum. You can also sing "Mighty To Save" by Hillsong, "Our God Saves" by Paul Baloche, "All To him" by The Desperation Band, Chris Tomlin's version of the hymn "When I Survey The Wondrous Cross," called "The Wonderful Cross" (co-authored by J.D. Walt, Jesse Reeves, and Lowell Mason), the hymn "Jesus Paid It All" by Elvina Mabel Hall and John Thomas Grape, or the hymn "Now I Belong To Jesus" by Norman John Clayton. (Chord charts are available at www.TransitionsWorship.com).

50 DAYS OF WORSHIP

DAY 19
The Game Of Life

WHEN I WAS a kid, I enjoyed playing the game LIFE, so a couple of months ago we purchased the new version of this game for our kids. Immediately, I noticed some things that were quite different from the version I played while growing up.

First, there are nine lawsuit spaces spread throughout the board that allow you to sue another player to the tune of $100,000. Of course, as you play the game, you are hoping to land on one of those spaces, because they are one of the biggest payouts. As a result, I had to have a little talk with my kids about lawsuits, reminding them that Romans 12 tells us to live at peace with all people. In fact, as we went through the game, I had to address a number of other issues with my kids concerning changes to the game that I did not appreciate, like the nine "Spin to Win," spaces, which is LIFE's version of the lottery.

As I reflected on it, I realized that most of the spaces on the board were characterized by selfish pursuits, and very few featured selfless activities. In fact, I counted twenty-three selfish pursuits, including things like a $5,000 college spring break vacation, $20,000 for the best seats at the big game, $30,000 for a sailboat, all the way up to $100,000 for cosmetic surgery. In the entire game, I only counted six spaces that could even be considered self-sacrificing. These were things like volunteering at a soup kitchen, learning sign language, adopting a pet, and donating to an orphanage. The selfish pursuits totaled $695,000, while the selfless pursuits totaled just $40,000. Not one space was connected with church or religion except for when it comes time to get married. And even then it's pretty much a drive-thru wedding, where you pull up to the white plastic church building and plug your pink or blue stick-figure spouse into your convertible. Although the church building sits next to the marriage space, there is no mention of the church in the game.

One of the most disturbing spaces in the game is located about two-thirds of the way around the board. It is an orange space where you are forced to stop because a fork in the road indicates that you have to make a decision about which path to take in life. One choice on this space says, "Continue on the path of life." It becomes evident from the wording for this choice and the opportunities this choice affords that this is the "normal" choice, where you can purchase a home gym for $30,000, a sports car for another $30,000, and get a pay raise. The second option is clearly the abnormal choice, which is labeled as "the family path," where you have the opportunity to have four more children. It is clear that if you want to win the game, you should not take the family path. This runs contrary to Psalm 127, which says that children are a reward from the Lord.

In the end, who wins the game? The person with the most money and the most toys. Well, that hasn't really changed from the original, but Jesus shows us the truth in Matthew 16:26 when he says,

"What good will it be for someone to gain the whole world, yet forfeit their soul?"

The question is, what is most important to you in the real game of life? You can sit in a church service and sing worship songs and claim to love God more than anything else, but your actions reveal your heart. How do you spend your money? How do you spend your time? What is important to you? So many Christians just want to live the normal American lifestyle, acquiring and consuming, but God calls us to take the "abnormal" path.

Jesus was so different than everyone expected him to be. Jesus took normal and turned it upside down. He touched lepers when everyone else avoided them. He hung out with people he wasn't supposed to be around—children, tax collectors, prostitutes, and sinners. The people around him thought success was everything, but Jesus said that if we want to win, we have to lose. If we want to live, we have to take up our cross and die.

Jesus didn't play the game of life like everyone else expected.

What kind of example are we setting for our kids by the way we play the real game of life? If they follow in our footsteps, will they be headed in the direction of Jesus? God didn't call us to hit the bull's eye in worldly success. In his book *Weird,* Craig Groeschel says, "If we raise our children to become well-adjusted, materially comfortable, professionally successful adults, but they don't know the One who created them or live for him, then all the success in the world is for nothing." Psalm 127 tells us that sons are like arrows in the hands of a warrior. What if we're pointing our arrows in the wrong direction?

Don't become so well-adjusted to your culture that you fit into it without even thinking. Instead, fix your attention on God. You'll be changed from the inside out. Readily recognize what he wants from you, and quickly respond to it. Unlike the culture around you, always dragging you down to its level of immaturity, God brings the best out of you, develops well-formed maturity in you. (Romans 12:2, *The Message*)

Who will you follow: the world and its desires that pass away or God and his will for your life (1 John 2:17)? If you are serious about transforming your worship, then it is important to play the game of life differently than our culture. If you want to take a stand, to live a counter-cultural (or, in biblical terms, *holy*) life and treasure what God values, sing "I Will Follow" by Chris Tomlin, Jason Ingram, and Reuben Morgan as a prayer of commitment.

Transition Through Reflection...

Read Matthew 7:13–14. Which path in life have you chosen to take? If you claim to be traveling the "narrow road," how is your life different than someone who has chosen the "broad road"? Take a few minutes to journal some ways that your life as a worshipper of the true and living God should look different from those around you. Spend time asking God to help you take the path less traveled.

1. _____

_____

2. _____

_____

3. _____

_____

4. _____

_____

5. _____

6. _____

7. _____

8. _____

9. _____

10. _____

Suggested Songs

Sing "Everyday" by Joel Houston of Hillsong, "From The Inside Out" by Joel Houston of Hillsong, the hymn "I Have Decided To Follow Jesus" by Sadhu Sundar Singh or the hymn "All The Way My Savior Leads Me." Chris Tomlin has a nice version of this Fanny Jane Crosby hymn on his "Hello Love" album, co-authored by Matt Redman and Robert Lowry. (Chord charts are available at www.TransitionsWorship.com).

DAY 20

Singing Or Silence

I HAVE BEEN A worship leader for the last eighteen years. As much as I love leading God's people in worship, it can also be a very discouraging job, because it is probably the only job in the church where a leader is held responsible for the congregation's response.

Think about it: The teaching pastor is not admonished if he preaches on tithing and the tithe does not increase in subsequent weeks. However, when there is a lack of participation or enthusiasm during musical worship, some church leaders have alleged that the burden of responsibility should fall on the worship leader. Maybe he is deficient in his song selection, musical style, or articulation. Maybe it's the way he dresses or the instrumentation.

I am fairly certain that Peter or James would have come to wildly different conclusions than many of our church leaders, who subscribe to "Attractional" models of church growth. Imagine the believers assembling in the temple courts for worship, prayer, and teaching in

Acts 2. More than 3,000 believers had been baptized and joined the apostles at this point. If Peter noticed that some of those who had gathered were not participating or were half-hearted as they praised God, do you suppose he would set up a meeting with those leading worship to find out what they were doing wrong? Instead, I believe the clear assumption would be that these "worship scrooges" were not true believers—or at least not giving Jesus their all.

If you consider the corporate worship at your church to be subpar, stop looking at the person or team on the platform and examine your own heart and what you believe about God. I highly doubt there were any worship wars in the first century church.

True believers who understand what worship is about will eventually conclude that they can worship in any situation and under any circumstances that do not conflict with biblical principles.

"I prefer the Psalms."

"No, hymns are deeper."

"None of them compare to spiritual songs because they have 'spiritual' in the title."

When people choose not to participate in corporate worship, to me, this indicates what they truly believe about God, not what they believe about the skill of their worship leader. This is an indictment of me as much as it is of anyone else, because I am just as much a product of our modern "have it your way" Christian culture. Worship is not about you, so stop making it about you and your preferences. Worship is a response to God's character and goodness.

I find it interesting to see the distinct response to God's message by two saints in Luke 1. The angel Gabriel appears first to Zechariah to share the exciting news that he and Elizabeth would have a son in their old age. Zechariah responds in unbelief, asking, "How can I be sure of this? I am an old man and my wife is well along in years" (v. 18). Gabriel is less than thrilled with Zechariah's response and declares,

I am Gabriel. I stand in the presence of God, and I have been sent to speak to you and to tell you this good news. And now you will be silent and not able to speak until the day this happens, because you did not believe my words, which will come true at their appointed time" (v. 19–20).

It is perfectly acceptable to ask sincere questions of God to better understand what he wants for your life. However, in Zechariah's case, his heart attitude was one of disbelief in God's promise. Zechariah's response should have been one of thanksgiving and praise at hearing such news. Instead, he was silenced because of his unbelief.

The very next account in Luke 1 is Gabriel's visit to Mary. Gabriel shares the incredible news that Mary will be the mother of God's Son. Unlike Zechariah, Mary responds in faith, saying, "I am the Lord's servant... May your word to me be fulfilled." Her song of praise, known as the "Magnificat" accentuates her response of faith. While Zechariah's unbelief resulted in silence, Mary's faith resulted in worship.

I believe that many times, silence is the response of unbelief. Don't get me wrong, sometimes we should be silent before God (e.g. Ecclesiastes 5:1–3), but as Ecclesiastes 3:7 indicates, there is "a time to be silent and a time to speak." Our corporate worship is a time when our faith should overflow in praise of God. Certainly an authentic worshipper can reflect on a worship song in the recesses of his or her mind, but when we are silent because we just don't feel like singing, it's probably due to a lack of faith.

If we truly believe we are entering the presence of the indescribable, all-powerful, creator God in a special way when we gather together in his name (Matthew 18:20), then how could we refuse to join the multitudes of Christ-followers who are lifting their voices in worship? I submit to you that among the silent majority may be a spirit of unbelief. When distraction or annoyance results in silence, maybe in that moment, you do not truly believe what you claim to believe, that Jesus is among us and is worthy of our praise.

Worship with the song "How Can I Keep From Singing" by Chris Tomlin, Ed Cash, and Matt Redman as you confess with the words of the man in Luke 9:24, "I do believe; help me overcome my unbelief!"

Transition through Application...

Have you enjoyed the stories and lessons in this book so far but refrained from participating in the exercises or singing the songs out loud? If so, you're not alone. I confess that I have a tendency to skim through books in order to gain some knowledge and then check it off my to-do-list. When I encounter requests from the author to be introspective and answer questions about myself, many times I skip over them. However, the purpose of this book is not to entertain you with clever stories or amaze you with deep insights but to help you encounter God through worship. Therefore, please do not be silent! If you have been skipping through parts of the book, I challenge you to go back to the sections you know you bypassed and use this book as an opportunity to respond to God with your entire being. Lift your voice in faith to the only One who is worthy of your worship.

Suggested Songs

Sing "Shout To The North" by Martin Smith of Delirious, "Everything" by Jason Wade of Lifehouse, or the version of "Sing We The King Who Is Coming To Reign" called "Sing To The King" by Billy Foote (popularized by Passion). (Chord charts are available at www.TransitionsWorship.com).

DAY 21
Presents In The Lobby

ONE DECEMBER MY church organized a Christmas gift donation project. We set up a Christmas tree in our lobby, where our church family could drop off toys to give to children in the inner city. By the middle of December, probably fifty presents were underneath the tree.

The children's ministries meet downstairs, so my kids had not yet seen this massive pile of Christmas cheer. One Sunday after our church service, my son Gibson, who was seven at the time, rode the elevator up to the lobby and made his initial discovery of the Christmas present gold mine. Astonished by the sheer glory of what lay before him, he asked my friend, "Who are these presents for?"

Without skipping a beat my friend responded, "They're for your brother, Taylor."

"Oh wow, that's swell! I'm so glad Taylor has been so abundantly blessed," Gibson replied.

Actually, that was far from Gibson's response to the prospect of his nine-year-old brother receiving fifty presents. You can probably guess what Gibson's actual reaction was like. He was horrified that his brother might get something and he would be left out. Understand: Here is a kid who has everything. Video games, action figures, Beyblades, Pokémon, you name it. They have to invent presents each year just so we have something different to buy for Christmas, and yet it never satisfies. He sees fifty presents under the tree and wants more. I don't mean to throw Gibson under the bus, because I am just as easily consumed by stuff, especially when I think I deserve more.

At the time, I lived about fifteen minutes from church, because we could not afford to live in the same town where our church was located. All the while my friends from church, with nice corporate jobs, were moving into that upper middle-class neighborhood. Whenever I drove to work, I admired the "McMansions" along my route and wished we could afford to sing our song of celebration along with the Jeffersons: "Well we're movin' on up, to the east side. To a de-luxe apartment in the sky. Movin' on up, to the east side. We finally got a piece of the pie!" This went on for a while until one day the Holy Spirit opened my eyes to the possibility of someone driving by my house and thinking, "I wish we could afford to move into a nice house like that."

> I struggle just like my seven-year-old to appreciate what I have been given and to choose contentment. It really is a choice.

I need to remind myself that I don't deserve more. In fact, I deserve less, but God has been gracious to me. I need to remember the words of James 1:17, which says, "Every good and perfect gift is from above, coming down from the Father of the heavenly lights…" Every good thing I have is a gift from God, and it is enough.

Transition Through Reflection…

I can only imagine how it grieves the heart of our Heavenly Father when we are not satisfied with his generosity. Take a few minutes to confess specific instances when you have coveted the blessings of your brothers and sisters and have not been satisfied in God alone. Then read Hebrews 13:1–6 and Philippians 4:10–13. As a way of expressing your contentment with God's provision in your life, write down several blessings he has bestowed on your friends and family, and then spend a few minutes in prayer thanking God for these things.

1. _____

_____

2. _____

_____

3. _____

_____

4. _____

_____

5. _____

_____

6. _____

_____

7. _____

_____

8. _____

_____

9. _____

_____

10. _____

_____

Suggested Songs

After you spend a few minutes telling God that he is all you need, sing "We Will Worship You" by Carlos Whittaker and Jason Ingram. You can also sing, "Enough" by Chris Tomlin and Louie Giglio, "You Are My All In All" by Dennis Jernigan, "Seek Ye First" by Karen Lafferty, or the hymn "Great Is Thy Faithfulness" by Thomas Chisholm and William M. Runyan. (Chord charts are available at www. TransitionsWorship.com).

50 DAYS OF WORSHIP

Hiding Place

A FEW MONTHS BEFORE my daughter Trinity's third birthday, my wife walked around the corner into our dining room and found Trinity and Jaylea hiding out behind the dining room table. Before you read on, go to the following YouTube link (https://www.youtube.com/watch?v=krVX73ZuN5w) or do a YouTube search for "Trinity's drug of choice" and watch the forty-eight second clip of my daughters.

That's right, Trinity's drug of choice is… Parmesan cheese! That didn't look too good, sucking it down with the straw. However, Trinity knew exactly what she was doing, even as a two-year-old. She grabbed the Parmesan off the counter and hid behind the table with it so she could enjoy her guilty pleasure in secret.

We all have "Parmesan" in our lives. It may not be as obvious as my daughter's addiction, because our drug of choice blends in with that of everyone else. But every single one of us is trying to fill a void in our lives with something other than God. Some of us try to fill it with actual drugs, sex, and partying. Others try to fill the void with things that are a little easier to excuse, because they are so common, such as money, power, entertainment, food, careers, families, or Parmesan cheese! These things can be good, except if they take God's place in our lives. When we hear a list like that, many of us think of someone else, but what about you? Have you been hiding behind the table recently, hoping that no one will notice you back there?

A few days after the Parmesan incident, I found someone else hiding in our house. I had looked everywhere for my wife, but I couldn't find her. I didn't call her name, because our house is small. Instead, I just walked into the few rooms where I expected her to be.

After striking out a few times, I entered our bedroom and found her lying on the floor behind our bed. When I asked what she was doing, she said she was trying to get away from everyone so that she could spend time talking with God. I think this is the true test, don't you? Are you hiding behind the table or lying on the floor behind the bed?

What do you do when no one is looking to catch you or to give you credit?

Matthew 6:6 says, "But when you pray, go into your room, close the door and pray to your Father, who is unseen. Then your Father, who sees what is done in secret, will reward you." If you truly want to transform your worship, run hard after Jesus, treating him as a person and not a program. Cultivate your friendship with him, enjoy him, and meet with him often, remembering that worship is our total response to God in faith. Psalm 37:4 says, "Take delight in the LORD, and he will give you the desires of your heart." If you are willing to sing this song as a prayer, ask God to change your heart's desires.

Transition through Application...

Read Psalm 32. If you have something on your heart that you need to confess today, kneel down beside your kitchen table and confess your sins to God. If you need to find a hiding place to simply communicate with your Father, then kneel down behind your bed. Thank God for being your only refuge and hiding place. "Sing, all you who are upright in heart!" (Psalm 32:11).

Suggested Songs

Sing "In The Secret (I Want To Know You)" by Andy Park. You can also sing "Enough" by Chris Tomlin and Louie Giglio; "Hiding Place" by Jared Anderson of New Life Worship and the Desperation Band; "Lord, I Need You" by Christy Nockels, Daniel Carson, Jesse Reeves, Kristian Stanfill, and Matt Maher (popularized by Chris Tomlin); or the hymn "Rock of Ages Cleft for Me" by Augustus Montague Toplady and Thomas Hastings. (Chord charts are available at www.TransitionsWorship.com).

DAY 23

Wave To The Clown

EVEN AS AN adult, I feel the need to act cool. I care too much about what other people think of me. I knew this about myself already, but it became even more obvious one morning as I was driving to our church service.

When I drove past a restaurant, I was confronted by a clown who waved at me and all the other motorists. I felt an obligation, perhaps even a desire, to wave back, but considering the well known fact that adults don't wave at clowns, I fixed my eyes on the road and continued on to my destination, immune to the clown's persuasive powers.

As I passed him, I chided myself. Why not wave to the clown? Am I so self-important and concerned about what others think that I need to pretend I don't see the guy with the large orange Afro?

I know it's inconsequential whether I wave at clowns as I drive past. The point of this story is not to try to get you to high five Chuck E. Cheese the next time you take your kids to play some video games. My point is, sometimes I think we have this same mindset when it comes to worship. Concerned about what the people around us will think, instead of giving God our all, we hold back.

Maybe you think you have a bad voice. Maybe you're concerned that others will misinterpret your motives, or maybe you don't want your friends to see you doing the "white man's overbite dance."

But God is seeking worshipers who are more concerned with what he thinks than what everyone around them thinks.

The goal of my worship team is not to put on a great show or to provide a free concert. It is to lead people to God's throne in unashamed worship. John 12:42–43 says, "Many even among the leaders believed in him. But because of the Pharisees they would not openly acknowledge their faith for fear they would be put out of the synagogue; for they loved human praise more than praise from God."

God is looking for worshippers like King David who danced before the Lord and said, "I will become even more undignified than this, and I will be humiliated in my own eyes" (2 Samuel 6:22). Are you one of them?

Transition through Application...

Are you willing to worship like King David? Are you willing to worship in a way that might make you feel insecure? Maybe that means raising your hands or bowing down. Maybe it simply means singing loudly to let your voice be heard, or perhaps it involves bowing your head in silence as you stand in awe of Jesus.

Read Galatians 1:6–10. Whose approval are you seeking when you worship?

Would you consider walking out on your front porch or front lawn and singing your song of worship? "But someone might hear me." Yes, that is the point. Have your neighbors ever heard you lift up your voice in unashamed worship? Will you become even more undignified? How?

_____

_____

It is rarely undignified to live in the land of your comfort zone. Break out today and worship God in a new way!

Suggested Songs

Sing "Undignified" by Matt Redman. You can also sing "I Am Free" by Jon Egan (popularized by the Newsboys), "I Could Sing Of Your Love Forever" by Martin Smith, or the hymn "Be Thou My Vision" by Eleanor Henrietta Hull and Mary Elizabeth Byrne. (Chord charts are available at www. TransitionsWorship.com).

DAY 24

We're Still Open

WHEN I DROVE by a church in my hometown recently, the message on their sign caught my attention. It replayed over and over in my mind on the way home, because it was the most depressing message I have ever seen on a church sign. What was the message? "We're Still Open."

As a church, if you have to tell people you are still open, you might as well close down, because you have become irrelevant. If people can't tell you're open because you are a light in the darkness, then writing it on a sign isn't going to help.

Their sign made me wonder about my own church. If we closed our doors tomorrow, would we be missed? What about your church? Would your town be worse off if your church did not exist, or would people even notice it was gone?

Sometimes it is easy to judge an entire organization, but what about you, personally? Have you made such an important impact in your church or community that people would notice if you were missing in action? Here is the big question: Would your absence from the worship service cause God to take notice?

Seeing as God is omniscient, I realize he is going to know if you are there or not, but that is not my question. You might respond automatically with, "Of course, God is just pleased I'm here." But look at what God said to the people in Malachi's day.

The question is: Does your contribution to the community of worshippers enhance God's pleasure as he receives your worship?

"Oh, that one of you would shut the temple doors, so that you would not light useless fires on my altar! I am not pleased with you," says the LORD Almighty, 'and I will accept no offering from your hands. My name will be great among the nations, from where the sun rises to where it sets ... and you say, "What a burden!' and you sniff at it contemptuously,' says the Lord Almighty." (Malachi 1:10–11a, 13)

Can you imagine God wishing a church would just close its doors? The goal of true worship is to make God's name great across this globe. Do you want to be a part of this incredible calling? The Israelites of Malachi's day did not want to give God the sacrifice or the worship he deserved. Instead, they decided to give him half-hearted, lukewarm worship. Did you notice how God described their attitude in verse 13? "And you say, 'What a burden!'" Is that your attitude as you attend a church service week after week? Do you find yourself saying, "Is it nearly over?"

Worship leaders have the unique vantage point of looking out on everyone as they worship, so we get to see the expressions and actions of the worshippers. One time I saw someone read a book throughout the entire service. Another teenager at my church was texting throughout the sermon. I had his number but he didn't have mine, so I pulled out my phone and texted him a message: "Stop texting – from God." On another occasion, a friend of mine was preparing to leave for vacation, and she spent an entire service creating a list of all the things she needed to bring with her.

Will you worship God the way he deserves to be worshipped? Will you engage your mind and focus on him for just a few minutes? Let the world see Jesus living in you through worship, and I guarantee you will be missed when you are absent, not only by other worshipers but also by God.

Transition Through Application...

Read Matthew 5:13–16. Have you shone so brightly for Jesus in your neighborhood that if you moved away, your neighbors would go through withdrawal? Or do you pull in your driveway or garage and head right into the house so that your neighbors would have to see a "We're still open" sign to even know you still live there?

Think about one thing you can do for one of your neighbors to show them Jesus' love. Maybe it's taking their garbage cans in from the curb, mowing their lawn, leaving an encouraging note in their mailbox. Write down an idea here, and then put this book down and go do it. Once you come back, take a few minutes to thank God for the privilege of being his hands, feet, and voice.

Suggested Songs

Worship our Savior by singing "Mighty To Save" by Ben Fielding and Reuben Morgan of Hillsong. Focus on the bridge, which says, "Shine your light and let the whole world see, we're singing for the glory of the risen King." You can also sing "Solution" by Joel Houston and Matt Crocker of Hillsong, "Make Me A Servant" by Kelly Willard, "Think About His Love" by Walt Harrah, or the hymn "Take My Life And Let It Be" by Frances Ridley Havergal and Henri Abraham Cesar Malan. (Chord charts are available at www.TransitionsWorship.com).

50 DAYS OF WORSHIP

Worship Equals Prayer

EACH WEEK, I have the privilege of receiving a review of our worship service from my wife. I say this with all sincerity, because Leah is a tremendous encouragement to me, but she will also speak the truth in love when she believes I can make some improvements as I lead God's people.

Recently, Leah told me that she doesn't think we spend enough time in prayer at our church, specifically prayers of adoration. I agree with her to an extent, because we often over-emphasize musical worship and under-emphasize spoken worship. But I also realized I had not done an adequate job of instructing our congregation about the true nature of musical worship. I needed to help them understand that worship songs can also be prayers of adoration. When we sing a song, we should sing it as if we are praying the words to God.

We don't just sing as filler for the service. Instead, we express prayers of adoration through music.

After recording many songs of praise that David wrote to God, Psalm 72:20 ends with, "This concludes the *prayers* of David son of Jesse." David called all of his worship songs "prayers." Songs are one of the most powerful ways to express our love in words. This doesn't just apply to worship songs either. A 2011 study showed that 92 percent of all songs that make the Billboard top 100 chart are love songs.

I am a singer, so I have sung songs to a few love interests in my lifetime. In high school, I took a page out of the blockbuster movie *Top Gun* and sang, "You've Lost That Loving Feeling," karaoke style, to a girl I met at the county fair. It was pretty embarrassing and lame as I look back on it. Undaunted, shortly after I graduated college, I penned a love song to the girl I was dating. I took her to dinner at Peddler's Village, which is an 18th century-style shopping and restaurant attraction. After dinner, we went for a walk, where I had my guitar stashed behind a bush. I grabbed it and sang her my love song in the midst of the crowded walkway. I also wrote a love song for my wife and sang it to her in front of 300 people on our wedding day.

If you don't have any musical talent, then you may have at least made a mix tape for the one you love (if you grew up in the 80s like me) or a playlist (if you're under 20). We often express our love using songs, because it is such a powerful medium, especially when the song says precisely what we would like to say to our loved one. Therefore, when Christians, worship we often do so by praying prayers of adoration in song, just like David.

Transition Through Reflection...

Sometimes it helps me to pray the "big idea" of a worship song in my own words and without the music before I sing it. Take a few minutes to reflect on the words of the song "Your Love Is Extravagant" by Darrell Evans (popularized by Casting Crowns). You'll note the words of this song sound more like a love song than a worship song. I have heard people criticize this style of "romantic" worship, but it seems to me that God often uses romantic language and themes in Scripture, such as the bride imagery in Ephesians 5 and Revelation 19. I believe God is "romantic," but his love for us is by no means limited to romance. People seem to have strong opinions on this topic, so without diving into the definition of romance or the nature of God's romantic love, I think we can agree that we were created with a desire for intimacy. Therefore, I believe the use of nonsexual but romantic imagery, similar to that expressed in the song "Your Love Is Extravagant," Psalm 63, and other psalms is a legitimate expression of worship.

If you desire to dig deeper into this expression of God's love for his people, I encourage you to do a study in the book of Hosea, specifically chapter 2. To be honest, as a man, this romantic imagery makes me uncomfortable, but in order to transform our worship, we must be willing to transcend our comfort zones. Therefore, using your own words, express the "big idea" of this song to God in prayer.

Your love is extravagant
Your friendship, it is intimate
I feel like moving to the rhythm of your grace
Your fragrance is intoxicating in our secret place
Your love is extravagant

Spread wide in the arms of Christ is the love that covers sin
No greater love have I ever known
You considered me a friend
Capture my heart again

Capture my heart again
Your love is extravagant
Your friendship, it is intimate

After you have prayed this song in your own words, sing it out loud as a prayer of adoration. Take these words and make them your own. If you are self-conscious about singing out loud, just remember the crazy things we do when we are in love. We want to shout it out so that everyone knows how we feel. Does Jesus deserve any less?

Suggested Songs

Sing "In The Secret (I Want To Know You)" by Andy Park or "Draw Me Close" by Kelly Carpenter (popularized by Michael W. Smith). (Chord charts are available at www.TransitionsWorship.com).

50 DAYS OF WORSHIP

DAY 26

Where O Death Is Your Victory?

I REALIZE THAT IT can be difficult sometimes to get the words out as we sing songs of worship. So many difficulties in life tend to drag us down. Is the weight of tragedy pulling you down in this season of life? Even though suffering abounds, God is good, and he often reminds us of how he cares for us. He did that for me recently.

A few weeks ago, I had a strange dream about my Uncle Carey. It was especially odd, because I haven't seen him in years. It's just one of those unfortunate realities of life. The busyness of my immediate family, the demands of church ministry, and complications from my uncle's medical condition (Frontal Lobe Dementia, similar to severe Alzheimer's) had kept us apart for far too long.

Through the ravaging effects of this terrible disease, Uncle Carey's mental faculties began to decrease rapidly starting at the age of 61.

Carey had not been able to recognize family members or speak coherent sentences for a number of years. Praise God that Uncle Carey was absolutely a believer in Jesus Christ and walking with Jesus long before the effects of Dementia set in.

In my dream, I went to visit Carey at the care facility in which he resided. As I approached the building, I noticed he was sitting outside enjoying the fresh air. Realizing that he would not recognize me, I walked toward him and greeted him with a lively "Hey, Uncle Carey!" anyway.

He turned toward the sound of my voice. "Oh, hi, Jason."

I was completely shocked, not only that he recognized me but also that he was able to speak a coherent sentence. The dream went on for a while longer, but when I woke up, that was the only detail of my visit that stuck.

The dream was encouraging, because it reminded me that, ultimately, this disease will not define Uncle Carey's existence. Dementia will be defeated, along with Alzheimer's, cancer, AIDS, diabetes, depression, Down Syndrome, MS, and every other affliction. One day, Uncle Carey will know the promise of 1 Corinthians 15:55–57 firsthand: "Where, O death, is your victory? Where, O death, is your sting?" The sting of death is sin, and the power of sin is the law. But thanks be to God! He gives us the victory through our Lord Jesus Christ." Death no longer holds us hostage, because God has given us the victory over death, sin, and disease.

I woke up to my alarm clock blaring. I got my kids ready for school and then headed over to my office. On the way there, I received a phone call from my mom, who informed me that Uncle Carey had passed away the previous night!

I don't often have "Twilight Zone" experiences like this, but I was thankful for God's reminder through the dream that death has no victory. It has no sting, because sin and death were defeated on the cross. All true worshippers of Jesus Christ will take part in this victory that Uncle Carey knows in a brand new way today as he encounters his Savior with full mental capacity.

As you sing 1 Corinthians 15:55–57, remember that whatever ailment, tragic situation, or sadness has gripped your heart has been defeated through the power of the cross. Jesus has given you the secret to being content in every situation.

It is his victory over sin and death that gives us hope for the future; guaranteeing deliverance from whatever seems so overwhelming in your life right now.

Transition Through Reflection...

Read Matthew 11:2–3. Why would John ask a question like this? What circumstances had caused John to doubt Jesus?

_____

_____

_____

Have any circumstances in your life caused you to doubt Jesus? What are they?

_____

_____

_____

Read John 1:29–34. How could John doubt after this experience?

_____

_____

_____

Go back to Matthew 11 and read verses 4–6. How does Jesus reassure John?

_____

_____

_____

What makes God's grace tough to see in your present circumstances? What events can you look back on that remind you of his faithfulness?

1. _____

_____

2. _____

_____

3. _____

_____

4. _____

_____

5. _____

_____

Spend a few minutes worshipping God using prayers of thanksgiving for his past blessings and our future hope.

Suggested Songs

Celebrate Christ's victory by singing Matt Maher and Mia Fieldes' song "Christ Is Risen." You can also sing "I Will Rise" by Chris Tomlin, Jesse Reeves, Louie Giglio, and Matt Maher; "Saving One" by Tim Neufeld and Jon Neufeld of Starfield; "God Is Able" by Ben Fielding and Reuben Morgan of Hillsong; "One Thing Remains (Your Love Never Fails)" by Brian Johnson, Christa Black Gifford, and Jeremy Riddle (popularized by Jesus Culture); the hymn "Victory In Jesus" by E.M. Bartlett; or the hymn "Christ The Lord Is Risen Today" by Charles Wesley and Samuel Arnold, focusing on verse three. (Chord charts are available at www.TransitionsWorship.com).

DAY 27

The Song No One Could Learn

RECENTLY, I DISCOVERED a passage in Revelation about worship that had gone unnoticed in my Bible study.

Then I looked, and there before me was the Lamb, standing on Mount Zion, and with him 144,000 who had his name and his Father's name written on their foreheads. And I heard a sound from heaven like the roar of rushing waters and like a loud peal of thunder. The sound I heard was like that of harpists playing their harps. And they sang a new song before the throne and before the four living creatures and the elders. No one could learn the song except the 144,000 who had been redeemed from the earth. (Revelation 14:1–3)

How cool is that? This was a song that no one could learn except this select group of people. Now, I realize you may read this and think, "What's the big deal? My worship leader does this to me every month! He tries to teach us a song that no one can learn!"

Nevertheless, this is the only place in Revelation where a song or hymn is mentioned but not quoted. Maybe John did this to prevent anyone from trying to learn it, since Revelation 14 described future events. The Greek term *learn* (μανθάνειν) used here could be the ordinary sense of "to learn, to be instructed," but it could also refer to the ability "to understand" a higher, more mysterious type of knowledge.

If the latter sense of *learn* is closer to the author's intention, there is an interesting parallel in 2 Corinthians 12:4, where Paul claims that someone (probably himself) was caught up to the third heaven and that "he heard things that cannot be told, which a person may not utter." Like the 144,000, Paul heard something in heaven that was impossible or inappropriate for others to hear or understand.

A common misconception is that, in heaven, we will have perfect knowledge and understanding. However, most of us will not know how to sing this particular song even in heaven. Not even the angels know everything. Despite being higher than humans, they are still capable of learning new things. First Peter 1:11 indicates that the prophets were seeking to understand the nature of the gospel in greater detail. Verse 12 goes on to say, "Even angels long to look into these things." Only God is omniscient. Neither humans nor angels will ever be omniscient.

Even in the perfection of eternal life, the distinction between the all-powerful, all-knowing Lord and his creation is vast.

Highlighting this, in his book *The Knowledge of the Holy*, A.W. Tozer says,

> Forever God stands apart, in light unapproachable. He is as high above an archangel as above a caterpillar, for the gulf that separates the archangel from the caterpillar is but finite, while the gulf between God and the archangel is infinite. The caterpillar and the archangel, though far removed from each other in the scale of created things, are nevertheless one in that they are alike created. They both belong in the category of that which- is-not-God and are separated from God by infinitude itself.

We have an amazing God whom we cannot even begin to understand. Songs are sung to him that most created beings cannot learn or understand. He is a God who turned water into wine and opened the eyes of the blind. He is greater, stronger, and higher than any other! There is no one like you, God!

Transition Through Reflection...

Did you ever struggle with a particular subject in school? I struggled with languages in high school, college, and in seminary. That side of my brain must not work as well as the other side, because I did well in many other subjects. So I certainly hope, in contrast to what I wrote above, that God zaps at least some knowledge into our brains when we enter heaven, because I do not want to have to sit through Mrs. Garcia's 9th grade Spanish class again before I can stand around the throne and worship with the "great multitude... from every nation, tribe, people and language" (Revelation 7:9).

My second son Gibson is now in fifth grade, so I am living that popular game show, "Are You Smarter Than A Fifth Grader?" There are times when he opens his homework, and I have no idea where to begin helping him. It is easier to acknowledge our limitations when we cannot understand something that others can understand. Therefore, take a few minutes to try and recall some areas of learning that have been difficult for you.

1. _____

_____

2. _____

_____

3. _____

_____

4. _____

_____

5. _____

_____

We worship a God who does not have a learning disability. He is perfect in his knowledge, and his ways are higher than our ways (Isaiah 55:9). If you are dealing with situations that you cannot understand, realize that God knows better than you do, and nothing goes unnoticed by him. Take a few minutes to tell him about a hardship that you do not understand and then ask him to give you "the Spirit of wisdom and revelation, so that you may know him better" (Ephesians 1:17).

Suggested Songs

Celebrate the greatness of our Lord through the song "Our God" by Chris Tomlin, Jesse Reeves, Jonas Myrin, and Matt Redman. You can also sing "Indescribable" by Jesse Reeves and Laura Story (popularized by Chris Tomlin), "God of Wonders" by Steve Hindalong and Marc Byrd (popularized by Third Day), "Where The Love Lasts Forever" by Joel Houston of Hillsong, or the hymn "How Great Thou Art" by Stuart Wesley Keene Hine. (Chord charts are available at www.TransitionsWorship.com).

DAY 28
The Candy Tax

A FEW DAYS BEFORE Halloween, my kids attended a party at their school and came home with a jackpot of candy. At the time, my son Taylor was ten years old. He spread his candy all over the floor, separating it into groups, as kids often do. My wife asked Taylor which candies he wanted to contribute to the "Mommy and Daddy candy tax." I wanted a piece of chocolate, but even though he had a lot of candy, he had only a few chocolate bars. He wanted to give me a chintzy jawbreaker or one of the other lame varieties of gumball machine candy.

"How about a Reese's?" I asked (because that's my favorite) "Or a Milky Way?" (Because who doesn't like a Milky Way?)

To my dismay, Taylor wasn't willing to part with any candy bars. I attempted to reach a compromise and asked for a simple mini Hershey Bar. Sadly, in defiance to my chocolate craving, Taylor's resolve remained unyielding.

My six-year-old daughter Jaylea, who had been sitting nearby, overheard the conversation and skipped over to me. "Here, Daddy." She handed me a Hershey bar.

I responded with a big, "Wow! Thanks honey!" Then I made a pronouncement to all those within earshot, "Jaylea is a really nice girl!"

Just as I started to walk away, Taylor said, "Nice girl? She just gave you *my* candy!"

It's easy to give something away that doesn't belong to you, isn't it? When we have the opportunity to worship God through our tithes and offerings, it helps to understand that our wealth doesn't belong to us anyway. When we realize that we are just stewards of God's resources, it's a lot easier to give away his things. Check out what God said to the Israelites about this in Deuteronomy 8:10–14, 17–18.

> When you have eaten and are satisfied, praise the Lord your God for the good land he has given you. Be careful that you do not forget the Lord your God, failing to observe his commands, his laws and his decrees that I am giving you this day. Otherwise, when you eat and are satisfied, when you build fine houses and settle down, and when your herds and flocks grow large and your silver and gold increase and all you have is multiplied, then your heart will become proud and you will forget the Lord your God, who brought you out of Egypt, out of the land of slavery... You may say to yourself, "My power and the strength of my hands have produced this wealth for me." But remember the Lord your God, for *it is he who gives you the ability to produce wealth.*

Everything we have comes from God, even our ability to produce wealth.

Transition through Application...

Read 2 Samuel 24:18–25. Did you notice David's description of worship? He would not give the Lord something that cost him

When you understand that God is the source, it is much easier to give him what belongs to him anyway.

nothing. Worship is costly, but many of us tend to be stingy with God.

If you struggle to give God what he deserves, spend a few minutes in prayer and ask him to change your heart. Perhaps it is time to commit to a ten percent tithe, especially if that would be a significant sacrifice. I have heard many Christians claim that we are no longer under the law; therefore, the Old Testament tithe does not apply. However, grace always goes beyond the law. The New Testament virtue of generosity does not stop with a particular percentage. As a part of worship, generosity must include complete submission of our entire selves, our total response to God in faith. That doesn't sound like something you can max out. However, I would certainly feel like I was being stingy with God if my giving fell below ten percent.

If you are among the few who regularly give to the Lord of your time, talent, and treasure, can you think of something more that God may desire of you? Do you give out of your abundance or out of your poverty? Invite God to reveal a specific sacrificial gift that you can give this week and make a note of it here. Remember, it all belongs to him anyway, so give cheerfully and without fear!

Suggested Songs

Take some time to worship God through the sacrifice of giving. As you do, sing "Give Me Jesus" by Jeremy Camp. You can also sing "More Precious Than Silver" by Lynn DeShazo, "You Are My All In All" by Dennis Jernigan, or the hymn "I'd Rather Have Jesus" by George Beverly Shea and Rhea F. Miller. (Chord charts are available at www.TransitionsWorship.com).

50 DAYS OF WORSHIP

DAY 29

Your Love Or His Love?

THE APOSTLE JOHN had an awesome nickname. John 19:25–26 reads, "Near the cross of Jesus stood his mother... When Jesus saw his mother there, and *the disciple whom he loved* standing nearby, he said to his mother, 'Dear woman, here is your son.'" No other gospel account uses this title for John, but the author of the gospel of John uses it six times. How did John get this title? Since no other New Testament author uses it, it seems likely that John gave it to himself. That raises a question: Are you allowed to give yourself a nickname?

It's similar to Indiana Jones giving himself the nickname "Indiana." His actual name was Henry Jones, Jr. He didn't like to be called "Junior," so he took on the nickname "Indiana," which happened to be the name of the family dog! You see something similar in *Bill And Ted's Excellent Adventure.* If Bill can give himself the title "Esquire," can't we all just make up our own titles or nicknames? (If you have no idea who Bill is, that's okay. Just let all the children of the 80s enjoy the flashback).

Wouldn't you like to be cool enough to give yourself your own title? I would probably call myself "the story-telling disciple" or maybe "the disciple who dominated church softball." Imagine having the title, "the disciple Jesus loved." Wouldn't that be cool?

I have given myself many job titles while working for small companies and churches. When I copied medical records for my mom's company, I called myself a "Copy Technician." When I started working in a church of eighty members after graduating college, I changed my title two times. I started out as the "Youth Director." After ordination, I became the "Youth Pastor." Years later, when I was the only employee for a two-year stretch, I changed my title to "Pastor of Student Ministries."

When you think about it, every follower of Jesus can take the nickname "the disciple Jesus loves" if they want it. We try to impress people with how much we love God instead of simply accepting his love for us. There's nothing wrong with saying we love Jesus, but we should be keenly aware of the outcome of Peter's many expressions of love for Jesus and his good intentions.

> The problem is, we often focus more on our love for Jesus than on his love for us.

After the last supper, Jesus predicted Peter's denial. In Mark 14:27–30, Jesus said, "You will all fall away." Peter responded by saying,

> "Even if all fall away, I will not." "I tell you the truth," Jesus answered, "today—yes, tonight—before the rooster crows twice you yourself will disown me three times." But Peter insisted emphatically, "Even if I have to die with you, I will never disown you."

Prior to his restoration, Peter tended to focus on his love for Jesus. John, on the other hand, seems to put the emphasis on Jesus' love for him. John certainly wasn't perfect, but he was the only disciple bold enough to approach the cross when Jesus was crucified. It is certainly not wrong to say you love Jesus, but think about how much more powerful your testimony will be if it draws attention to Jesus' love for you rather than your love for him.

After Jesus rose from the dead, he met with Peter, and the following conversation ensued: "'Simon son of John, do you truly love me?' he answered, 'Yes, Lord, you know that I love you'" (John 21:16). It is difficult to get a sense for what is happening here in our English translations, because we only have one word for "love." This dialogue is even more interesting in Greek, because there are different words for love that express distinct nuances of this verb. Jesus' question was actually, "Peter, do you *agape* me?" *Agape* is the purest, greatest form of self-sacrificial love. Peter answered Jesus by saying, "Yes Jesus, you know that I *phileo* you." Peter was admitting that he loved Jesus with a lesser, brotherly love. Jesus asks this question three times. Peter is sad when Jesus asks him the third time, because it is evident that Jesus is drawing a parallel to his three denials. Jesus is clearly restoring him even as he embraces his brokenness.

Peter came to realize that he had overestimated his love for Christ, but isn't it great that we can never overestimate God's love for us? So let's concentrate on his love for us. Let's tell others about his love for us and glory in his love for us. Many worship songs focus on our love for Jesus, and it is certainly not wrong to sing such songs, but as we do, we need to remember that although our love for Jesus may waver, his love for us does not.

Have you ever overestimated your love for someone? If you've had a boyfriend or girlfriend that you did not marry, then you may have overestimated your love in a big way. In fact, many people have experienced painful break-ups, where the expression of their feelings toward a boyfriend or girlfriend has quickly deteriorated from extreme love to extreme hatred (Jeremiah 17:9). If we cannot trust the quality of our love in regard to human relationships, how can we place so much confidence in our love when it relates to Jesus?

The only reason we have to trust our love is because God's love makes our love possible. 1 John 4:19 says, "We love because he first loved us." The strength of our love is fully dependent on Jesus' love for us, and since we can be certain that his love is unfailing, I believe it is acceptable to declare our love for Jesus. However, it is more appropriate, and certainly more inspiring to a love-deprived generation, to focus on Jesus' perfect love rather than our imperfect affections.

Transition through Application...

Read Romans 8:31–39. This passage indicates the strength of Jesus' love for you. In your opinion, what is the most striking feature of this description of his love?

_____

_____

_____

Make a list of some other things included in "anything else in all creation" that are not able to separate you from Jesus' love.

1. _____

2. _____

3. _____

4. _____
_____

5. _____
_____

6. _____
_____

7. _____
_____

8. _____
_____

9. _____
_____

10. _____
_____

Are you willing to declare Jesus' love this week in a radical way by changing or adding a personal signature to all your text messages that says, "Jesus loves you – want to know more?"

You can set up a personal signature that will automatically be integrated into all of your text messages. On your smart phone, go to your text message app and find the settings. From there, look for settings for outgoing messages, and you should be able to add the suggested message or anything else you are inspired to include.

If that is too difficult to figure out, then you can fake it by just typing those words at the end of each text; thereby fooling your friends into thinking you are tech savvy. I challenge you to do this for one week and see what kind of response you get.

Suggested Songs

If you want to transform your worship, focus on Jesus' longsuffering, measureless love for you today by singing the hymn "The Love Of God" by Frederick Martin Lehman and Meir Ben Isaac Nehorai. (Mercy Me has a nice version of this hymn.) You can also sing "Amazed" by Jared Anderson of Desperation Band; "One Thing Remains (Your Love Never Fails)" by Brian Johnson, Christa Black Gifford, and Jeremy Riddle (popularized by Jesus Culture); "Your Love Oh Lord" by Brad Avery, David Carr, Mac Powell, Mark D. Lee, and Tai Anderson of Third Day; or the hymn "Jesus Loves Even Me" by Philip Paul Bliss. (Chord charts are available at www.TransitionsWorship.com).

50 DAYS OF WORSHIP

DAY 30
Pulling Weeds

W E REQUIRE OUR children to do a few chores each day, but they can also do a few extra things to earn some Chuck E. Cheese dough. One such opportunity is weeding the yard. My wife pays them a penny per weed, which might seem stingy on our part, but for a kid it can be quite a lucrative business.

One day, Taylor, who was seven at the time, was out working in the yard, and my wife poked her head out the door to check on him. She noticed that, instead of pulling weeds, he seemed to be burying something.

"What are you doing, buddy?"

In a matter-of-fact way Taylor said, "Oh, I'm planting seeds from the dandelions to make sure I'll always have a job."

Taylor's version of serving his father and mother is very similar to the way we serve our Heavenly Father at times. We serve and worship in expectation of a reward rather than simply out of love for our Father.

In fact, an entire movement within Christianity has been founded on a rewards-based theology. Called the "health and wealth gospel," it promises God's physical and financial blessings when our faith is great enough to serve God generously. Usually, that act of faith comes in the form of a large donation to a particular ministry. This isn't the gospel; it's completely contrary to the gospel.

If Taylor weeded with the love of his parents at the forefront of his mind, he would never plant dandelion seeds. In the same way, trying to manipulate your Father in order to obtain rewards is not love. Proverbs 16:2 says, "All a man's ways seem innocent to him, but motives are weighed by the Lord." God searches our inner being, judging the thoughts, attitudes, and motives of our heart. We tend to go easy on ourselves, assuming our motives are pure. So take a minute to evaluate your love for your Father through his eyes, to the extent that is possible. How would you describe your love for him? Would you want your child to serve you the way you serve Jesus?

_____

_____

_____

_____

_____

_____

_____

Transition Through Reflection...

Why do you serve God? Is it for the reward or do you do it in gratitude for who he is and what he has done? Manipulation, greed, and consumerism lead to narcissism, not love. 1 John 4:19 says, "We love because he first loved us." Our love is a response to Jesus' incredible love for us! That is worship: our total response to God in faith.

Read Matthew 13:24–30, 36–43. Who sows the weeds in verse 25?

_____

_____

_____

_____

_____

How does Jesus describe the weeds in verse 41?

Do you come to church, sing worship songs, and give your tithe because you hope that God will bless you, or do you do it because he has already blessed you?

_____

_____

_____

_____

Do you plant weeds or do you sow righteousness? Since we have yet to reach perfection (Philippians 3:12), write down a few examples of how you have planted weeds in God's garden. Then spend a few minutes asking God to pull those weeds out of your life.

1. _____

_____

2. _____

_____

3. _____

_____

4. _____

_____

5. _____

_____

Suggested Songs

Worship God by singing the hymn "Come Ye Sinners, Poor And Needy" by Joseph Hart and William Owen. Andrew Threlkeld, Billy Smiley, and Maggie Amini have an updated version of this hymn called "Come Ye Sinners" (popularized by Todd Agnew). If you do not know the melody, spend a few minutes reflecting on the lyrics. You can also sing, "Glory To God Forever" by Steve Fee and Vicky Beeching, "U.R.Y." by Kate Wray (Spence) (popularized by Hillsong), the hymn "My Jesus I Love Thee" by Adoniram Judson Gordon and William Ralph Featherstone, or the hymn "I Am Thine O Lord" by Fanny Jane Crosby and William Howard Doane. (Chord charts are available at www.TransitionsWorship.com).

50 DAYS OF WORSHIP

DAY 31

Will You Show Up?

A FEW YEARS AGO, I took our youth group to a stadium conference event. It was one of those weekend conferences that they reproduce all over the country. I visited the conference website and mistakenly assumed that the Christian bands that were listed would perform at all of the locations. Only later did I find out that this was not the case.

Based on my faulty assumptions, I created a poster for the event and advertised it to my students, incorrectly promoting a number of really good bands that were not actually performing.

I was awfully disappointed that only a handful of students attended the conference, especially considering our unintentional false advertising. Out of frustration with our students I sarcastically said to one of our youth staff members, "I bet if we advertised that Jesus was going to be there we would still only have a few students show up."

Those of us who did go on the trip had an amazing weekend, because even though most of our youth group didn't show up, Jesus did. Lives were changed, because Jesus' presence was evident.

We know that Jesus is omnipresent, which means he is not limited to one location in time and space as we are, but we long for a more personal connection with our Savior. The thing you need to remember is that Jesus wants to join your church service, Bible study, or accountability group in a special way. You don't have to wait for him to show up; he is already there! Matthew 18:20 says "For where two or three come together in my name, there I am with them." If the people of your church have gathered in Jesus' name, then he is with you in a personal, special way.

In Matthew 23:37 Jesus said, "Jerusalem, Jerusalem, you who kill the prophets and stone those sent to you, how often I have longed to gather your children together, as a hen gathers her chicks under her wings, and you were not willing." Just as Jesus wanted to gather the inhabitants of Jerusalem to pull them close, he desires a relationship of intimacy with all his children.

Although we know Jesus will show up, the real question is, will you show up?

You may think, "But Jason, I go to worship services every week, so of course I show up." Just ask your husband, wife, mom, dad or best friend if you have ever been present without really showing up—such as when they try to have a conversation with you while you are watching the TV or chatting online with others. Will you "show up" at your church service this week? You can transition from singer to worshipper simply by engaging your mind and focusing on Jesus.

Transition through Application...

Read Hebrews 13:5. If you have accepted Jesus Christ as your Savior and put your faith in his sacrifice on the cross for your sins, then you can be certain that Jesus is always with you. Even if you feel alone at this moment, Jesus promises he will not leave you. Are you showing up for him? Have you engaged Jesus personally with your presence this week? If so, how?

_____

_____

_____

_____

_____

Jesus wants to connect with you through his Word. If you desire to connect with him, read the rest of Hebrews 13. List some of the things you find in Hebrews 13 that you can do this week to connect with Jesus in the spirit of Matthew 25:40: "I tell you the truth, whatever you did for one of the least of these brothers of mine, you did for me."

1. _____

_____

2. _____

_____

3. _____

_____

4. _____

_____

5. _____

_____

6. _____

_____

7. _____

_____

8. _____

_____

Suggested Songs

As you sing "Meet With Me" by Lamont Hiebert, ask Jesus to meet with you today in a personal way through his Word, through worship, and through prayer. "Come, Now Is The Time To Worship" by Brian Doerksen is a good alternative as you focus on engaging your mind in worship. You can also sing "Be Near" by Shane Barnard or the hymn "In The Garden" by Charles Austin Miles. (Chord charts are available at www.TransitionsWorship.com).

50 DAYS OF WORSHIP

Backbiting Worshippers

P SALM 15:1–3 SAYS,

LORD, who may abide in Your tabernacle? Who may dwell in Your holy hill? He who walks uprightly, And works righteousness, And speaks the truth in his heart; He who does not backbite with his tongue, Nor does evil to his neighbor, Nor does he take up a reproach against his friend." (NKJV)

"Backbiting" is not part of the vocabulary of most English speakers these days. Sometimes it used as a synonym for gossip, but it carries the distinct sense of flattering someone in their presence and then slandering the person when he or she is not around. A "backbiter" pretends to be a friend to your face, but he or she kicks you when you turn your back.

At the age of ten, my son Taylor lost a tooth. He put it in a Ziploc bag for safekeeping for the tooth fairy, but he forgot about it, leaving the bag on the kitchen counter.

The next morning, Leah was preparing school lunches and didn't notice the tooth in the Ziploc bag. So she filled the bag with popcorn and put it into Taylor's lunch box.

Later that day, Taylor was enjoying the popcorn at school when he bit into something hard. Thinking it was an un-popped kernel; he pulled it out of his mouth. Needless to say, Taylor was shocked that instead of a popcorn kernel, it was a tooth. And not just any tooth—the same one he had lost the day before! The worst part of the story is that Taylor was sharing his popcorn with his friends at the lunch table. Yuck!

This strikes me as a funny illustration of a literal form of backbiting. One day Taylor was using that tooth to bite, and then the next day, his own tooth bit him back. The biblical use of backbiting is similar, where someone who is a friend one day turns into a foe the next. James 3:9–10 says,

> With the tongue we praise our Lord and Father, and with it we curse human beings, who have been made in God's likeness. Out of the same mouth come praise and cursing. My brothers and sisters, this should not be.

In essence, we slander God's name by calling ourselves Christians but not living out our faith. We praise God to his face and then dishonor him when we think he's not looking. Of course, he is always looking, but many times we live as though we do not really believe that is true (Psalm 139:7–8).

Sadly, I think that, at times, our worship is just like backbiting. We sing God's praises as we sit in church, but then we don't live it the rest of the week.

194

Have you ever sung a song like "Crown Him With Many Crowns" on Sunday and then yanked the throne of your life right out from under Jesus as you walked out of the service? God does not want our lip service on Sunday and then the backbiting of our actions Monday through Saturday. He deserves authenticity at all times. If you desire to be an authentic worshiper, don't just sing the words "Crown Him With Many Crowns," strive to live those words this week.

Transition through Application…

Read the rest of James 3 to learn more about honoring God with your mouth. Then use the chart below to make a list of ways that we sin using our tongue. Next to each category of the sins of the tongue, write an example of how you have used your tongue to hurt others and to dishonor God. Spend some time confessing those sins if you have not done so. Then take a magic marker and write over top of those sin categories (in the left column), describing how you can use your tongue to honor God. For example, over "lying" you can write "honesty." Next to each example of how you used your tongue in a sinful way, brainstorm how you can use your tongue to honor God the next time you are in a similar situation.

SINS OF THE TONGUE	I HAVE USED MY TONGUE TO HURT OTHERS BY…	INSTEAD, I CAN USE MY TONGUE TO HONOR GOD BY…

Suggested Songs

Chris Tomlin has a nice version of "Crown Him With Many Crowns" called "Crown Him (Majesty)" on his Burning Lights album (co-authored by Ed Cash and Matt Maher). You can also sing "We Crown You" by Eddie Kirkland and Steve Fee, "You Are God Alone" by Billy J. Foote and Cindy Foote (popularized by Philips, Craig, and Dean), or "Everyday" by Joel Houston of Hillsong. (Chord charts are available at www.TransitionsWorship.com).

50 DAYS OF WORSHIP

DAY 33
Flag People

PEOPLE COME UP with all kinds of different ideas to worship God. I've seen some worship styles that are just not my thing, but I do appreciate when people use their God-given creativity to worship him in unique ways.

One such group of worshippers is the "flag people." Have you ever been around worshippers who wave flags during a church service? I don't know if they are leftovers from the high school marching band or air traffic controllers looking for some other outlet for their talents, but I appreciate their enthusiasm. I've never had the impulse to wave a flag in worship, so I think it is God's sense of humor that I always seem to be standing next to a flag person when I go to a worship event. As I have learned from past experience, don't ever close your eyes while worshipping next to a flag person, because sometimes they close their eyes. Often, I end up ducking and diving out of the way, because they're so focused on worship that they fail to observe other people's personal space.

I may think the flag people are a little weird, but who cares what I think? They are not worshipping me, and hopefully they are not seeking approval from anyone but God. They seem to be worshipping God with all their might, and I admire them for that. I'm not saying you have to be a flag person to accomplish this, but you should be willing to do whatever God asks of you no matter what others think. John mentions that some Jews believed in Jesus but were afraid to acknowledge their faith for fear of the Pharisees, "For they loved human praise more than praise from God" (John 12:43). True worshippers are always more concerned with God's approval than the approval of their peers. This is easier said than done, because sometimes we will look ridiculous to those around us.

One of the greatest biblical examples of unashamed worship took place when David brought the Ark of the Covenant into Jerusalem. (For a reminder of what led to this moment in Jewish history, see "Day 1: Sincerity Versus Obedience.")

> Wearing a linen ephod, David was dancing before the Lord with all his might, while he and all Israel were bringing up the ark of the Lord with shouts and the sound of trumpets. As the ark of the Lord was entering the City of David, Michal daughter of Saul watched from a window. And when she saw King David leaping and dancing before the Lord, she despised him in her heart. (2 Samuel 6:14–16)

Michal was David's first wife. First Samuel 18:20 says that Michal was in love with David. When David fled Jerusalem, because Saul was trying to kill him, Michal was taken away from David and given to another man. Eventually, David became king, and he demanded that Michal be returned. Their relationship may have been strained at this point, which could have contributed to Michal despising David. That is not clear from in the scriptural account, but what is clear is that Michal despised David because of how he worshipped God. Verse 20 indicates that Michal was embarrassed by David's expression of worship.

I know that David's wardrobe had something to do with her embarrassment, but I also wonder if David's dancing skills left much to be desired. If David qualified for "Dancing With The Stars" and looked like a stud out on the streets of Jerusalem, I don't think Michal would have been quite as embarrassed. He was unconcerned about what Michal thought of him, saying, "I will become even more undignified than this, and I will be humiliated in my own eyes" (v. 22). How many of us are not only willing to make that statement but also to live it?

Perhaps David was not a great dancer, but he was willing to go all-out in worship, undaunted by the opinions of others.

Transition through Application...

What physical expression of worship is God placing on your heart right now—lifting hands, bowing, dancing, or maybe even waving a flag?

_____

_____

Does anything about that expression of faith embarrass you? If so, how might you overcome that embarrassment?

_____

_____

Read Luke 9:23–26. Would you be embarrassed if your classmates, neighbors, or coworkers saw you living out your faith? Take some small steps to acknowledge Jesus in your workplace or at school this week. Consider carrying your Bible with you, bowing your head, and praying for your lunch. Or maybe you can sing a worship song at a time or place where worship songs are not typically sung.

I hope you will also have the opportunity to live out the Great Commission in one of those settings, proclaiming Paul's words in Romans 1:16, "For I am not ashamed of the gospel, because it is the power of God that brings salvation to everyone who believes."

Suggested Songs

Are you willing to transform your worship by becoming "more undignified" for the sake of bringing honor to Jesus Christ? If so, express your commitment by singing "Unashamed Love" by Lamont Hiebert. You can also sing "Undignified" by Matt Redman; "Sing, Sing, Sing" by Chris Tomlin, Daniel Carson, Jesse Reeves, Matt Gilder, and Travis Nunn; or the hymn "Be Thou My Vision" by Eleanor Henrietta Hull and Mary Elizabeth Byrne. (Chord charts are available at www.TransitionsWorship.com).

50 DAYS OF WORSHIP

DAY 34
Rejected Stone

ACCORDING TO MATTHEW 27:33, Jesus was crucified just outside the city walls of Jerusalem at a place called Golgotha, which means "the place of the skull."

Tradition indicates that Golgotha was originally a quarry where many of the limestone blocks used in Jerusalem were cut. A section of rock in the quarry was inferior and not useable as building stone, so the excavators left the second-rate stone where it was and continued cutting the good stone around it. This left a hill of rejected stone that resembled a skull. It reminds me of Matthew 21:42, which, quoting Psalm 118:2, says, "The stone the builders rejected has become the capstone; the Lord has done this and it is marvelous in our eyes." Jesus is the stone that was rejected, and he was crucified on a hillside of rejected stone.

In Matthew 27:43–44, Jesus goes on to say, "Therefore I tell you that the kingdom of God will be taken away from you and given to a people who will produce its fruit. He who falls on this stone will be broken to pieces, but he on whom it falls will be crushed." Jesus is saying that we need to throw ourselves on his mercy. Those who fall on the stone of Jesus Christ will be broken or humbled. They will die to themselves and live for Christ. However, those who do not humble themselves by confessing their sin and spiritual inadequacy will be crushed when the conquering King returns.

The Apostle Paul develops this theme further in Romans 9:31–33.

The acceptable response of worship of our risen Savior is to humble ourselves by admitting we are broken, fallen sinners in need of his grace.

Israel, who pursued a law of righteousness, has not attained it. Why not? Because they pursued it not by faith but as if it were by works. They stumbled over the "stumbling stone." As it is written: "See, I lay in Zion a stone that causes men to stumble and a rock that makes them fall, and the one who trusts in him will never be put to shame."

The Jews pursued good works in order to attain a right relationship with God and receive eternal life. Other than Christianity, this is what every single religion that has ever existed has taught, to some degree.

True Christians pursue righteousness through faith in God's grace instead of through good works. However, people have been tripped up by this truth. The gospel was offensive to the Jews and most other adherents of human-centered religions, because it claims that you aren't good enough and you need a savior. Think about it: What is the easiest way to offend someone? Tell the person that he or she is wrong. Those who fall on the stone are willing to admit that their way does not work. It is humbling to admit you are wrong and helpless. When you do so, your ego is broken to pieces. Worshipping God the way he desires to be worshipped is humbling. Sadly, most worshippers today are more interested in satisfying their wants and desires than humbling themselves.

I have had the opportunity to visit the Church of the Nativity in Bethlehem twice in my lifetime. The builders of this church understood this aspect of true worship. Worship is not something that is done in comfort, because humility is not comfortable. Therefore, it's like they designed the door of this church for hobbits. It's so low it forces men and women of average height to bow down and humble themselves before entering into the presence of God.

Have you fallen on this stone or will this stone fall on you?

Transition through Application...

Read Daniel 2:31-45. Daniel prophesied about what was going to happen to every human kingdom, institution, and belief system. The great rock that crushed Nebuchadnezzar's statue is Jesus Christ. All other religions and humanistic philosophies will be crushed, and the wind will sweep them away without leaving a trace, but the gospel of Jesus Christ will became a huge mountain that fills the entire earth. The gospel is far superior to all other religions, because it is true. Sadly, people will be crushed by it when they refuse to humble themselves and fall on God's mercy. How is your pride interfering with the humble worship that Jesus is seeking?

_____

_____

_____

_____

_____

_____

Take a few minutes to pray and throw yourself on the Stone and allow Jesus to begin (or continue) breaking your pride to pieces. God has given you a part to play in allowing this Rock to grow into a mountain. Has God placed someone on your heart who needs to hear about this ultimate truth? Do you know someone who is standing right in the path of the great meteor that is hurtling toward our worldly philosophies and religions, someone in danger of being crushed? Write the person's name in the space provided.

_____

_____

_____

_____

If you see disaster coming, take the opportunity to warn those around you as an act of humble worship before our great and glorious King.

Suggested Songs

Worship the Lord in humility by admitting that you need a savior and sing Hillsong's version of the hymn "My Hope Is Built (The Solid Rock)" called "Cornerstone" by Eric Liljero, Jonas Myrin, and Reuben Morgan. You can also sing "Counting On God" by Jared Anderson of Desperation Band, "How Sweet The Sound" by Ben Calhoun and Josh Calhoun of Citizen Way, "In Christ Alone" by Stuart Townsend and Keith Getty, or the traditional hymn "My Hope Is Built (Solid Rock)" by Edward Mote and William Batchelder Bradbury. (Chord charts are available at www.TransitionsWorship.com).

50 DAYS OF WORSHIP

DAY 35

Tattoos

D O YOU KNOW anyone who has made a really big tattoo mistake? I worked as a youth pastor for eighteen years, ten of which were in Philadelphia, so I have seen my fair share of really unwise teenage tattoos. I have seen guys get the name of their girlfriend tattooed on their arm. Not a good idea to do as a teenager. How many of those relationships actually work out? They end up with permanent body art that remains fashionable for about as long as their relationship lasted.

After I shared this at church, a guy came up to me and rolled up his sleeve. "I knew you were going to go there," he said as he showed me his ex-girlfriend's name tattooed on his arm from when he was eighteen years old. At this point he was about twenty-five and married to another woman. He had tattooed over his ex-girlfriend's name with a Jesus fish.

We see this a lot in Hollywood. One of the most famous is Angelina Jolie's tattoo of her second husband's name. If I could give any advice to the Hollywood elite, don't tattoo the name of your second, third, or fourth spouse on your arm. For a good laugh, do a Google image search for "tattoo mistakes." (Make sure your safe search filter is set to "strict" so you don't run into unwanted images.) Isaiah 49:16 says, "See, I have engraved you on the palms of my hands." God has your name tattooed on his hands. Isn't that awesome? John 10:28–29 says, "I give them eternal life, and they shall never perish; no one can snatch them out of my hand. My Father, who has given them to me, is greater than all; no one can snatch them out of my Father's hand." Your Heavenly Father doesn't just have your name written on his hands, he's using his hands to hold you tight as well.

God loves us so much that he has permanently engraved us on his hands.

Take some time to sing the old hymn "Before The Throne of God Above" by Charitie Lees Bancroft, especially the second verse of this song, which says, "My name is graven on his hand, my name is written on his heart."

Transition Through Reflection...

Read Romans 8:28–39. Who can separate you from the love of God?

_____

_____

_____

If you cannot be separated from the love of God, then what is there to fear in this life?

_____

_____

_____

How should this reality motivate you to live as a selfless worshipper?

Spend a few minutes in prayer, brainstorming with your Father about what it looks like to be an extreme worshipper. Ask him to move you closer to those aspirations.

Suggested Songs

Sing "The Power of the Cross" by Keith Getty and Stuart Townend; "Whom Shall I Fear (God Of Angel Armies)" by Chris Tomlin, Ed Cash, and Scott Cash; or "All Because Of Jesus" by Steve Fee (popularized by Casting Crowns). (Chord charts are available at www.TransitionsWorship.com).

DAY 36
Raise The White Flag

SURRENDER IS NOT viewed as a positive thing in our culture, because when an army surrenders, they lose the battle. Although as human beings, and especially as Americans, we don't like the idea of surrendering, the kingdom of God always turns things upside down. When you raise the white flag in God's Kingdom, you've won.

A verse that Christians often quote and use as their life verse is found in Jeremiah 29:11. "'For I know the plans I have for you,' declares the Lord, 'plans to prosper you and not to harm you, plans to give you hope and a future.'" Interestingly, Jeremiah relates this message from God while the people of Judah are captives in the land of Babylon. The people of Judah rejected God and his law, so God allowed them to be conquered by King Nebuchadnezzar and deported to Babylon. Jeremiah advised Judah's king to surrender to Nebuchadnezzar so he and the people of Judah would live and prosper. Although false prophets were predicting that Judah would break the yoke of Babylonian captivity within two years, Jeremiah prophesied that the people would remain exiled for seventy years. He told the exiles to surrender completely, even encouraging them to pray for the prosperity of Babylon, saying, "if it prospers, you too will prosper" (Jeremiah 29:7b). God's plan to prosper his people was in the context of surrender. In fact, God's plan to prosper his people is always in the context of surrender.

Read Mark 9. In verse 35, Jesus said, "Anyone who wants to be first must be the very last, and the servant of all." In Romans 12:1, Paul tells us what true worship is all about: "Therefore, I urge you, brothers and sisters, in view of God's mercy, to offer your bodies as a living sacrifice, holy and pleasing to God—this is your true and proper worship."

Worship is dying to self and living for Christ. It is submitting to his will. When we raise the white flag, we win through the power of the cross.

Many distractions in our world keep us focused on things rather than on God. Instead of turning our blessings into idols, we need to think about how we can surrender our time, talent, and treasure for God's glory.

Transition Through Reflection...

As you worship God today, grab a white T-shirt or dishtowel and a stick and create a makeshift flag. What part of your life or what blessing do you need to surrender to God?

Wave your flag as you sing the song "White Flag" by Chris Tomlin, Jason Ingram, Matt Maher, and Matt Redman. When you conclude your musical worship, express the thought conveyed in the song in your own words as a prayer to God. As you prepare to worship God in surrender, consider the following challenge I issued once to my church congregation.

"While we sing this song, I encourage you to take a stand this morning by making your way to the front of the auditorium and waving one of these flags as a symbol of your surrender. Each flag has a different symbol on it. You can wave this flag with the clock on it to say, 'Jesus, I want to give you more of my time.' Or you can wave this flag with the moneybag to say, 'Jesus, I submit my finances to your will.' Here's a tough one: 'Jesus, I tend to lose my temper when I play sports or I usually play sports for my glory and not yours and I want to surrender my talent to you.' You can also surrender your education, career, technology, or home. And here is a blank flag if none of the symbols fit what God has put on your heart. Come forward, wave the flag, and then lay it at the foot of the cross. The same flag can be used multiple times, so just pick it up, wave it, and return it. Even if you are not moved to come forward and take this stand in front of your church family, I would still like you to make a commitment in your heart to use a specific blessing for the glory of God and raise your voice as we sing to make your inward commitment known."

Suggested Songs

Sing, "Surrender" by Dave Lubben, "Surrender" by Marc James, or the hymn "I Surrender All" by Judson Wheeler Van DeVenter and Winfield Scott Weeden. (Chord charts are available at www. TransitionsWorship.com).

DAY 37
Strong Tower

HOW WOULD YOU like to be able to say you are a trillionaire? I am officially a trillionaire, because I ordered the Zimbabwe 100 trillion dollar bill on eBay!

Can you imagine if the United States had a 100 trillion dollar bill? At the height of Zimbabwe's hyperinflation in 2008–2009, 100 trillion dollars could barely purchase a cart of groceries. Do you think the people of Zimbabwe ever thought their economy would reach such lows—and the denominations on their bills such highs? Probably not. We live with the same false assurance in our economy, but if we're not careful, we could become trillionaires as well—and not in a good way!

All around us, our world is changing on a fundamental level. Businesses that were once "too big to fail" are collapsing. Even our expressions are changing. Think of "a penny saved is a penny earned," "the check's in the mail" or "you can take that to the bank." Will our children even understand what these mean?

Many of us trust in wealth that so easily comes and goes. In Proverbs 18:11 Solomon exclaimed, "A rich man's wealth is his strong city." I like what he says next: "And like a high wall in his own imagination."

Your wealth is a strong tower, but only in your own imagination.

In the previous verse, Solomon says, "The name of the LORD is a strong tower; the righteous run to it and are safe." In biblical times, towers were used for protection from enemies and thieves. They were built into city walls and even in vineyards as a place of refuge and to enable people to see enemies or thieves from far away. If someone attacked, people would flee into the tower for protection. Building on this idea, Solomon wants to remind us that God's name is secure. He is faithful! He is our refuge! He is our strong tower!

Transition Through Reflection...

Think of as many names for God as you can and write them in the space provided. Do some research on the Internet to find out the meaning of the names that you wrote. Read Psalm 61 and spend some time thanking God for being our refuge.

GOD'S NAME	MEANING

Suggested Songs

Worship God's power and glory as you sing "Your Name" by Glenn Packiam and Paul Baloche. You can also sing "Strong Tower" by Aaron Sprinkle, Jon Micah Sumrall, Marc Byrd, and Mark D. Lee (popularized by Kutless); "Blessed Be the Name of the Lord" by Clinton Utterbach; "You Are My All In All" by Dennis Jernigan; or the Hymn "A Mighty Fortress" by Frederick Henry Hedge and Martin Luther. (Chord charts are available at www. TransitionsWorship.com).

DAY 38
Perfume

ONE SUNDAY I planted an undercover "agent" at the main entrance to our auditorium as people arrived for our worship service. My confederate was armed with a bottle of Jován Musk, which happens to be my wife's favorite perfume (I confiscated it from our bathroom cabinet.) He sprayed the perfume all over his hand and then shook hands with as many people as possible as they entered the auditorium.

During our worship time, I said, "I have an unusual request for you. Please smell your right hand. Yes, I know this is a little strange, but humor me." If they smelled anything unexpected, I asked them to tell their neighbor about it. Then I explained what I had done and asked them to read 2 Corinthians 2:14–16.

> But thanks be to God, who always leads us in triumphal procession in Christ and through us spreads everywhere the fragrance of the knowledge of him. For we are to God

the aroma of Christ among those who are being saved and those who are perishing. To one we are the smell of death; to the other, the fragrance of life.

Are you the kind of Christian whose love cannot be silenced, not because you are so incredible but because you are in awe of the One who loved you when you were unlovable?

Jesus' love is contagious. In fact, 1 John 4:19 says, "We love because he first loved us." Are you a contagious Christian? When you are consistently looking up at your Father, others will "smell" his love in your eyes and in your life. Will you be the one who is unashamed in your worship and unashamed in your witness? Will you cause others to want to know this God because your love reeks of his love?

_____
_____
_____

Transition Through Reflection...

What keeps you from spreading the fragrance of the knowledge of Jesus everywhere you go?

_____
_____
_____
_____

Read Romans 1:8–17 and then take some time to pray verse 16 aloud in your own words.

If you're really bold, spray some perfume on your hand before you interact with your family members to remind you that Christ wants to spread the fragrance of the knowledge of himself through you!

If you want to transition from singer to worshiper, responding to God in faith, then you must take opportunities to spread the knowledge of Jesus.

Suggested Songs

Express your commitment to worship Jesus through carrying out the Great Commission by singing "To The Ends of The Earth" by Joel Houston and Marty Sampson of Hillsong. You can also sing "Unashamed Love" by Lamont Hiebert; "Tell The World" by Joel Houston, Jonathon Douglass, and Marty Sampson of Hillsong; or the hymn "I Love To Tell The Story" by Arabella Catherine Hankey and William Gustavus Fischer. (Chord charts are available at www. TransitionsWorship.com).

DAY 39

Blindness

IN ISAIAH 6:9–10, God says of the Israelites,

Be ever hearing, but never understanding; be ever seeing, but never perceiving.' Make the heart of this people calloused; make their ears dull and close their eyes. Otherwise they might see with their eyes, hear with their ears, understand with their hearts, and turn and be healed.

Jesus references this passage in Matthew 13, saying that it was a prophecy that was fulfilled when he spoke to the people in parables.

Now, read Revelation 3:14–22. I had the opportunity to take a trip to Turkey and visit the ruins of the seven churches of Revelation. In Laodicea, I learned that the people of this city manufactured a famous eye medicine that produced incredible wealth for their citizens. In AD 60, an earthquake destroyed the city, but they refused to receive help from Rome to rebuild. Their great wealth led them to believe they were self-sufficient. The Laodiceans did not need to rely on anyone, or so they thought. But Jesus says in verse 18, "I counsel you to buy from me... salve to put on your eyes, so you can see." The Laodiceans might have been able to help heal a person's physical eyes, but they could do nothing for their spiritual blindness. They were blind, because they relied on their own strength to save them. Thus, Jesus designates them as "lukewarm." In the same way he wanted to help them, Jesus wants to open our eyes and set us free.

Here is how I illustrated the concept of spiritual blindness to my church congregation. I started by telling them that those of us with good sight often take it for granted. Then I told everyone to close their eyes and try to shake hands with the person next to them. After having some fun with this, I told them to keep their eyes closed as we took our offering. "Just reach into your wallet, pull something out, and drop it in the plate." You wouldn't believe how many eyes flew open!

Transition Through Reflection...

Take the next five minutes to do some of your regular activities around your house with your eyes closed. It probably won't even take two minutes for you to realize how important sight is. You can make some big mistakes when your eyes are closed.

In light of this, I find it interesting that when Satan tempted Eve to eat the forbidden fruit, he said, "For God knows that when you eat from it your eyes will be opened, and you will be like God." Satan promised that their eyes would be opened, but in actuality this is where our spiritual blindness began. Ever since then we have been groping around in spiritual darkness. Our thinking has become futile and our foolish hearts are darkened (Romans 1:21). However, Jesus wants to remove our spiritual blindness with the truth.

Take some time to confess to God if you have been relying on your own sight for direction and enlightenment. Express your need to see from God's perspective. You need to lift your eyes to Jesus, because that is where your help comes from.

Suggested Songs

Read Psalm 121 and sing "I Lift My Eyes Up" by Brian Doerksen (popularized by Sonic Flood). You can also sing "Father Will You Come" by Ben Smith, Christian Paschall, and Pat Barrett of Unhindered; "Always" by Jason Ingram and Kristian Stanfill; or "Open The Eyes Of My Heart" by Paul Baloche. (Chord charts are available at www.TransitionsWorship.com).

Our worship is transformed when our trust in Jesus increases, so worship by fixing your eyes on him (Hebrews 12:2).

DAY 40

Smart Phone Picture Gallery

PULL OUT YOUR smart phone and open your picture gallery. Who is in most of your pictures? Most of us have picture galleries that are filled with people we see every day. Haven't you had enough of those people? Not when you truly love someone. You can't get enough of that person, right?

Do you know that this is how God thinks of you? Psalm 139:17–18 reads, "How precious are your thoughts about me, O God. They cannot be numbered! I can't even count them; they outnumber the grains of sand!" (NLT). I imagine that David is just saying God thinks about us a lot, but if we take that literally, and you live to be eighty years old, God will have thought about you 2.9 billion times per second! We don't really understand numbers like 1 billion, but to put it into perspective, approximately 1 billion seconds ago, it was 1983. Close to 1 billion minutes ago, Jesus demonstrated his love for us by hanging on a cross so that 1 billion hours, 1 billion days, and 1 billion years from now we can stand with David, Noah, Moses, and

Your picture is all over God's "smart phone," because he thinks about you constantly— and he never gets sick of you!

all the other saints enjoying the riches of God's glorious inheritance and basking in the glory of his presence.

Remember that next time you pull out your phone. *You* are God's wallpaper, and Jesus paid a high price for that "app." No, not application but *appeasing* the wrath of God. It cost him everything; he loves you that much! So worship God with thanksgiving, knowing he sees you through the righteousness of Christ according to who you are and will be, not who you were.

Transition Through Reflection...

Read Psalm 40:1–5. David says that God's wonders, deeds, and plans for us are too numerous to declare. Do you believe that? If so, declare out loud a few that come to mind and then write them down.

1. _____

2. _____

3. _____

4. _____

5. _____

6. _____

7. _____

8. _____

_____

9. _____

_____

10. _____

_____

Hopefully you needed extra room! Spend some time praising God in your own words for his love.

Suggested Songs

Sing "Hallelujah (Your Love Is Amazing)" by Brenton Brown and Brian Doerksen. You can also sing the hymn "The Love of God" by Frederick Martin Lehman and Meir Ben Isaac Nehorai (Mercy Me sings a popular version of this hymn), "Who Am I" by Mark Hall of Casting Crowns, "Amazed" by Jared Anderson of Desperation Band, or "You Are My King (Amazing Love)" by Billy J. Foote (popularized by the Newsboys). (Chord charts are available at www. TransitionsWorship.com).

DAY 41

Cardboard Testimonies

CARDBOARD TESTIMONIES ARE a phenomenon that was popularized by Hillside Christian Church in Amarillo, Texas. It involves people writing a two-part testimony on a cardboard sign, such as "Never knew a father's love... The Father's love made me an awesome dad!"

I put a slightly different spin on this idea by combining it with the worship song "Blessed Be Your Name" by Matt Redman. I asked fifteen people from my church to write something bad that happened in their lives on the front side of a 2' x 2' piece of cardboard and, on the other side, how God turned that situation around or used it for good. At the bottom of both sides the signs were emblazoned with these words: "Blessed be your Name."

As the congregation sang, people came forward to reveal their cardboard testimonies. The front side of my sign read, "November 2008, my grandpop passed away. Blessed be Your Name." Side two said, "Five months later, my daughter was born on his birthday. Blessed be Your Name." My wife's sign read, "Dad left when I was 16. Blessed be Your Name" and "God taught me how to forgive. Blessed be Your Name."

Job has his own version of a cardboard testimony. After losing everything, Job says, "Naked I came from my mother's womb, and naked I will depart. The Lord gave and the Lord has taken away; may the name of the Lord be praised" (Job 1:21). In his book *The Problem of Pain* C.S. Lewis said, "God whispers to us in our pleasures, speaks to us in our conscience, but shouts in our pains: It is his megaphone to rouse a deaf world." We tend to remember and are more likely to turn to God in the midst of tragedy, because we cry out to him in our pain. However, it is not often that we worship him despite our suffering as Job did. Praise was Job's natural response to tragedy, because it was part of the fabric of who he was.

> It is much easier to praise God when things are going great in life, but, sadly, we tend to forget about God in the midst of good times.

In February 2014, my family made a road trip to Orlando. After driving all night from Pennsylvania, we crossed into Florida at around 7:00am and stopped for breakfast at McDonalds.

Jaylea didn't want to join us in the restaurant, so she slept in the car with Leah while the rest of us scarfed down our McGriddles. That was our first indication that something was wrong with Jaylea.

When we arrived at our rental property, the other four kids immediately jumped into the pool, but Jaylea didn't feel up for Marco Polo. With five kids, influenza is a common occurrence throughout our year. Usually we default to Motrin and bed rest to conquer the flu, but over the course of the next three days, her health continued to worsen. Finally, Leah and I realized we needed to get her to the hospital.

The emergency room doctors ordered a CT scan immediately and found that her right lung was twenty percent filled with fluid and her left lung was 80 percent full. In essence, Jaylea was breathing on one lung only. Because her chest cavity was also filling with fluid, she was in respiratory distress, her lungs unable to expand fully. When the doctors suggested airlifting her to the children's hospital in Orlando, we realized her condition was critical.

The doctors at the children's hospital initiated a procedure to drain the fluid from her chest and then put Jaylea on a ventilator. They ran all the usual tests and determined she had the H1N1 "Swine Flu" virus and bacterial pneumonia.

After a week, Jaylea was worse then when we arrived, so the doctors suggested they implement their plan for surgery as a last ditch effort to relieve the pressure from the fluid amassing in her chest. The doctors told us that we would know if the surgery was successful within forty-eight hours. But almost two weeks after entering the intensive care unit, Jaylea showed no signs of improvement. Her condition was so serious that local ABC and Fox News affiliates carried her story. Moreover, upon returning home, we learned that the story had been broadcast nationally. Even a London newspaper had printed an article on Jaylea.

To prepare our hearts for the possibility of losing our daughter, Leah and I fell down in worship. To be honest, I did not feel like worshipping God at that moment, but it was this response to tragedy that carried us through. Throughout the process, I came to understand Job's decision to worship God in response to tragedy. I don't believe it was necessarily a decision to worship God despite tragedy, merely that worship was the only remedy to lift him from this extreme aguish. Holding onto that level of heartache will destroy you. Our only constructive solution is to give it to Jesus by expressing our trust in him through worship.

The doctors wanted to do a second surgery, but the surgeons thought Jaylea was showing a hint of improvement, so they suggested that the ventilator be removed to accelerate her recovery. It was a very difficult third week, but by God's grace, Jaylea turned the corner. Along the way, God gave Jaylea, my wife, and I the strength to go on as we continued to submit ourselves in worship.

As I write this chapter, Jaylea is ninety-nine percent recovered. Singing worship songs to our Lord and Savior Jesus Christ absolutely helped my little girl persevere through the difficult process of detoxing from the morphine, relearning how to walk, and enduring the breathing treatments. You can watch a seven-minute documentary of Jaylea's ordeal here: https://www.youtube.com/watch?v=Zsu6Dm4KwAc. Make sure you don't miss her singing "Whom Shall I Fear (God Of Angel Armies)" by Chris Tomlin, Ed Cash, and Scott Cash while receiving a breathing treatment.

I would not have chosen this type of challenging event for my family, but now that this trial is behind us, I would not trade it for anything, knowing how it developed perseverance in all of us. God gives, and he takes away, and he is worthy of praise as we receive and release what he has given. If you want to take your worship to a whole new level, respond to God in faith by declaring his goodness even in the midst of difficult circumstances.

Transition Through Reflection...

Read Romans 8:18–30 and spend a few minutes thanking God for the truth of verse 28. Then do a YouTube search for "cardboard testimonies" and watch one or two of the videos from churches around the country. Then write your own cardboard testimony. Try to think of a difficult situation that God used for your good and summarize the details on a piece of cardboard. Even though we may not be able to see it at the time, God blesses us through trials.

Suggested Songs

Sing "Blessed Be Your Name" by Beth Redman and Matt Redman. You could also sing the hymn "It Is Well" by Horatio Gates Spafford and Philip Paul Bliss. Finally, while you are on YouTube, search for he song "Blessings" by Laura Story and reflect on the lyrics as you listen to the music. (Chord charts are available at www.TransitionsWorship.com).

Wedding Vows

RECENTLY, I HEARD someone say that marriage vows create unrealistic expectations and false hopes. Some people feel like marriage vows should be eliminated from the wedding ceremony or at least modified to be more realistic. One Christian woman seriously suggested the following vow:

I _____ take thee, _____ to be my lawfully wedded wife/husband. I promise to do my best to love you to the best of my ability, and I expect you to do the same. If ever I stop trying to love you, or if ever you stop trying to love me, then we will seek marriage counseling immediately as a means of showing we hold our marriage in high regard. If, after counseling, either one of us is still not trying, then that will nullify these vows, which we made. It will mean that we have committed emotional infidelity. If, after counseling, we feel a renewal in our commitment to love one another, then we will continue on. This vow I make before God, who tells us that we should 'do unto others as we would have them do unto us' and that we should 'love our neighbor as ourselves.' By saying these vows, I am showing that I place you, as well as me, in high regard and that I will treat you with love and respect. In saying this vow to me, you will be declaring the same. May God bless our marriage.

The author of these vows also mentioned that marriage was never meant to be a "life sentence." It was meant to be a loving partnership. Wow, that is distressing. If you are not willing to proclaim, "'til death do us part," why get married in the first place?

Just as you must choose to love your spouse every day, you must also choose to worship God daily. Most of us would confess freely that we often fail to fulfill our vows. We do not love, comfort, and honor like we should or as we have promised. But is the solution to our inevitable failures to abandon vows altogether and replace them with wishy-washy assertions?

Unfortunately, this is exactly what I have heard some people promote concerning our worship songs and our love for God. We sing songs like "Everyday" by Hillsong and declare, "Everyday it's you I live for. Everyday I'll follow after you. Everyday I'll walk with you my Lord." Some say that we should not sing unrealistic words of commitment like these, because we will surely fall short. As W. Clement Stone said, "Aim for the moon. If you miss, you may hit a star."

We need to shoot for something better, and that is the intention inherent in these worship songs of commitment. If you know you will fall miserably short, as most of us do, then pray this song as a prayer and say, "Jesus, this is the kind of disciple I want to be. Help me live up to this commitment through your strength."

Transition through Application...

Read Psalm 101. This Psalm of commitment is one of the ways that David chose to worship God. Think of one commitment that you would like to make to God today, write it on this page, and then express it to God in prayer.

Fear of failure is not a legitimate excuse to shy away from declaring your commitment.

Suggested Songs

Sing "Everyday" by Joel Houston of Hillsong. You can also sing "Nothing Can Silence Our Love" by Jimmy Robeson, "You Are Holy (Prince Of Peace)" by Marc Imboden and Tammi Rhoton (popularized by Michael W. Smith), "Love The Lord" by Lincoln Brewster, or "I Will Follow" by Chris Tomlin, Jason Ingram, and Reuben Morgan. (Chord charts are available at www.TransitionsWorship.com).

DAY 43
Jars of Clay

WHEN I WAS a kid, I decided to save up all my allowance money for a new Huffy bicycle. At that time, most of my allowance money came in the form of quarters, so I had to find a place to stash a growing supply of change. As an eight or nine-year-old, I was concerned about thieves breaking in and stealing my savings—or at least thieves disguised as my younger brother or sister. I needed a container in which no one would expect to find my riches.

I settled on one of the gallon-sized plastic ice cream containers that my mom saved for leftovers. I put my change in the bucket and then hid the bucket in the back corner of the freezer. My logic may have been slightly faulty, because an ice cream container in the freezer probably gets more attention than most other things. But at least it was unlikely that real thieves would steal perishable items from the freezer. When no one was around, I would open the freezer, count my change, and then run my fingers through my cold, hard cash.

Check out what the Apostle Paul writes about treasure in 2 Corinthians 4:7: "But we have this treasure in jars of clay to show that this all-surpassing power is from God and not from us." In Paul's day, people did not have steel safes or banks to store their most valuable possessions. Instead, they used unassuming containers like clay jars or pots, similar to my ice cream bucket. They figured no one would suspect riches to be hidden in ordinary clay pots. Even though we may look ordinary on the outside, just like clay jars, we have a tremendous treasure hidden within. But rather than hide it from others, we have the incredible responsibility and privilege to share it with the world.

In the same way, we are simple, ordinary humans, but God chose to hide a priceless treasure within us: his love, his Spirit, and his message.

Transition through Application...

Read 2 Corinthians 4:1–7. What secret and shameful ways do you need to renounce today?

_____

_____

Take some time to confess any sin that has caused your light to dim. If you are a true follower of Jesus Christ, he has placed the light of the knowledge of the glory of God in you. Let it shine!

Spend a few minutes writing down several ways you can share the treasure of Christ's love with your community over the next month. Think of one or two specific actions you can take, because generalized commitments rarely materialize. Instead of writing, "God, I will obey you this month," write something like, "God, I will obey you this month by..." Remember, obedience to God is essential in transforming your worship.

1. _____
_____

2. _____
_____

3. _____
_____

4. _____
_____

5. _____
_____

Once you have completed your list of ways you can shine for Jesus this month, copy the list onto another piece of paper. Take your commitments and place it in a container around your house. Instead of using the container to hide your commitments, choose an ordinary location where it will be easily discovered by your family or roommates as a way to let your light shine. As you do, remember you are like that ordinary container that holds the precious treasure of God's own Spirit!

Suggested Songs

Express your commitment to share God's treasure by singing "Shine" by Matt Redman. You can also sing "Mighty to Save" by Ben Fielding and Reuben Morgan of Hillsong (start with the bridge), "Let It Shine" by David Leonard and Leslie Jordan of All Sons and Daughters, or the children's song "This Little Light Of Mine" by Harry Dixion Loes and Nancy R. (Gordon) Nesbitt. (Chord charts are available at www.TransitionsWorship.com).

DAY 44
Lifting Your Hands

MOST OF THE churches I have attended have not been characterized by expressive worship. In fact, the worship in my church traditions would better be described as subdued or, if you want to get spiritual, reverent.

As a worship leader, I tend to push the envelope, because I want people to understand that there are other valid expressions of worship. For instance, body language is a key component of all forms of communication, including worship. In his book *Silent Messages,* Dr. Albert Mehrabian, shares his research on nonverbal communication and concludes that only seven percent of our communication is conveyed through words. Ninety-three percent of any message is imparted through nonverbal cues. That sounds a bit high to me, but after a brief Internet search, it seems that most researchers agree that the percentage of nonverbal communication is higher than we expect and far surpasses verbal communication.

Knowing this, shouldn't we communicate with God the same way we do with other people? Here's the truth: We already are, whether we realize it or not. It is so easy to approach God and communicate our worship similar to how we recited the pledge of allegiance in grade school—with a blank stare and without a single thought to what we were actually communicating with our body language. Authenticity is very important when we come before God in worship. We can achieve this by focusing on the content of what we are singing, but we also need to focus on what we are communicating to God through non-verbal means. I believe this is one of the reasons why physical expressiveness has historically been very essential to true worship.

Likewise, our body language betrays us as our engagement in corporate worship—or lack thereof—is made evident.

In his book *Celebration of Discipline*, Richard J. Foster elaborates on the importance of embracing nonverbal expressions of worship.

> The Bible describes worship in physical terms. The root meaning for the Hebrew word we translate worship is "to prostrate." The word "bless" literally means "to kneel." Thanksgiving refers to "an extension of the hand." Throughout Scripture we find a variety of physical postures in connection with worship: lying prostrate, standing, kneeling, lifting the hands, clapping the hands, lifting the head, bowing the head, dancing, and wearing sackcloth and ashes. The point is that we are to offer God our bodies as well as all the rest of our being. Worship is appropriately physical.

One of the physical expressions of worship that Foster mentions is the lifting of hands. Raising our hands in worship is absolutely biblical. Psalm 134:2 says, "Lift up your hands in the sanctuary and praise the LORD." It is important to understand what we are communicating through the different postures of lifting our hands. Please remember that these outward expressions of worship are not intended to draw comparisons between you and other worshippers. There are many legitimate expressions of worship, so we should be careful not to judge our fellow worshippers and just focus on our own hearts.

Transition through Application...

Although Tim Hawkins could probably do a comedy bit about this worship expression, nevertheless, I would like you to use one of these hand-raising postures each day this week as an expression of worship during your devotional time. (As a disclaimer, other worship leaders, whose names I cannot recall, inspired some of these worship postures.)

I. We can express worship to God by holding our arms outstretched at chest level with palms facing upward. You can call this expression of worship "clean hands." When our younger children have made a mess of themselves at dinner, they are required to submit to inspection before they are allowed to leave the table. We don't want their grubby, little handprints all over the walls and furniture, so we make them hold out their hands so we can ensure they are clean. James 4:8 says, "Wash your hands, you sinners, and purify your hearts, you double-minded." God wants to purify us from all unrighteousness (1 John 1:9). We hold out our hands in confession so God can inspect our lives and make the necessary changes to cleanse us. Lamentations 3:40–42 says, "Let us examine our ways and test them, and let us return to the LORD. Let us lift up our hearts and our hands to God in heaven, and say: 'We have sinned and rebelled.'" Use this posture to lift your hands to God and sing "Give Us Clean Hands" by Charlie Hall.

2. You can express worship by holding your left hand at head level, palm facing outward. I refer to this posture as "testifying hands." Before someone testifies in court, the person places his or her right hand on the Bible and left hand in the air and swears to tell the whole truth and nothing but the truth. As Christians, we want to testify to the truthfulness of God's inspired Word. Psalm 119:47–48 reads, "For I delight in your commands because I love them. I lift up my hands to your commands, which I love, and I meditate on your decrees." Sing "Thy Word" by Amy Grant and Michel W. Smith while your hand is raised as an expression of your love for God's commands, remembering that Jesus said, "If you love me, keep my commands" (John 14:15).

3. The next hand-raising posture is the most basic. You hold your hands out at stomach level but near to your body with palms facing upward. Your hands should have a similar look to when you cup your hands together to hold water. When my children ask for candy, and I am feeling unusually generous, I ask them to cup their hands so that I can pour forth the sugary blessings. At those times, one hand will not do the job, so I ask them to hold out their "receiving hands." Do you trust that God wants to pour forth his blessings in your life? Psalm 63:1–5 reads,

> O God, you are my God, earnestly I seek you; my soul thirsts for you, my body longs for you, in a dry and weary land where there is no water. I have seen you in

the sanctuary and beheld your power and your glory. Because your love is better than life, my lips will glorify you. I will praise you as long as I live, and in your name *I will lift up my hands.* My soul will be satisfied as with the richest of foods; with singing lips my mouth will praise you.

If you do not come from a tradition of hand-raising in worship, I also refer to this particular hand posture as the "Hand-raising Starter Kit." This is the most inconspicuous form of hand-raising, so if you desire to increase your physical expressiveness in worship but you're concerned about drawing attention to yourself in a corporate setting, this is a good place to start. Worship God with this hand posture while singing the "Doxology." Gateway Worship has an alternative version of this song that I recommend called "New Doxology" by Thomas Miller.

4. In Exodus 34:20, God instructs his people in worship by saying, "No one is to appear before me empty-handed." Therefore, the fourth hand-raising posture is called "offering hands." As much as we enjoy receiving from the Lord, we need to remember that worship is more about giving than receiving (Acts 20:35). We do not come before the Lord in worship to see what we can get out of him but to give to him. Our worship services would look very different if we consistently came before the Lord with a sacrificial attitude. Hold your hands out at stomach level with your elbows at your side and your palms facing inward as if you were holding a gift. Assume this worship posture while you sing, "Surrender" by Marc James or the hymn "I Surrender All" by Judson Wheeler Van DeVenter and Winfield Scott Weeden.

5. The international sign of surrender is lifting your hands straight up over your head with palms facing outward. When enemy soldiers are captured, they lay down their weapons and lift their hands in surrender to show that they are no longer a threat. Psalm 28:2 says, "Hear my cry for mercy as I call to you for help, as I lift up my hands toward your Most Holy Place." We lift "surrendering hands" to God as we ask for his mercy. As you practice this worship posture, sing "The Stand" by Joel Houston of Hillsong or "White Flag" by Chris Tomlin, Jason Ingram, Matt Maher, and Matt Redman.

6. As a dad, this final hand-raising posture has a special place in my heart. As I am writing this, my son Parker is 10 months old. Parker isn't walking yet, so he will sit on the ground and lift his hands straight up over his head with palms turned inward expressing his desire to be picked up and held by his daddy. What an incredible feeling it is when my baby boy wants me to scoop him up in my arms! The song "Forever Reign" by Hillsong expresses the idea of "daddy hands" in the chorus. "Oh, I'm running to your arms, I'm running to your arms. The riches of your love will always be enough. Nothing compares to your embrace." As you lift your hands to your Father and sing "Forever Reign" by Jason Ingram and Reuben Morgan, reflect on Paul's words in Romans 8:15: "For you did not receive a spirit that makes you a slave again to fear, but you received the Spirit of sonship. And by him we cry, 'Abba, Father.'"

Take some time to think about additional worship postures that would be appropriate in worship and then use them to help your nonverbal communication in worship to catch up with your words. (Chord charts are available at www.TransitionsWorship.com).

The Holy Towel

THE WORD *HOLY* has sort of been lost in our modern language. We typically only use the word when we are in church. But holy actually means "to be set apart."

One of the *holiest* things I own is my bath towel. No one else is allowed to use it, because it is set apart for me alone. My towel obsession started a few years ago when we purchased our home. We only have one full bathroom for the eight of us. Unfortunately, this also means guests use the same bathroom where we take our showers.

After taking a shower in the morning, I would hang my towel on the hook behind the door in the bathroom so that it could dry. A few times after we had guests at our house, I went to the bathroom and found that even though we have a hand towel right next to the sink, people were using my towel to dry their hands. Well, that's it for that puppy! It went right into the wash. Because my towel is set apart for me alone, it is holy.

Knowing I don't like anyone else using my towel, as a joke, a few years ago my wife gave me a brown towel for Christmas with the words "Jason Only" embroidered in white lettering. Unfortunately, with the kind of friends I hang out with, it ends up being more of a challenge to desecrate my towel than a warning to stay away. Nevertheless, my towel is holy, because it is set apart.

This is what we are saying about God when we call him holy. God is set apart. He is completely different than you or me. He is perfect, he is beyond our understanding, and he is altogether distinct. In fact, this is his anthem. Angels stand around his throne and sing over and over, "Holy, holy, holy is the Lord God Almighty. Who was and is and is to come" (Revelation 4:8). Psalm 104:1–2 says, "Praise the LORD, my soul. LORD my God, you are very great; you are clothed with splendor and majesty. The LORD wraps himself in light as with a garment." We wrap ourselves in towels and blankets, but God wraps himself in light. He is clothed in splendor and majesty. Can you do that? Nope! Because he is set apart, he is holy!

When Moses entered God's presence, God instructed him to take off his shoes, because he was standing on holy ground. I've often wondered: why shoes? I've been in people's homes where they have asked guests to remove their shoes. I don't like to remove my shoes, because my feet are not the most desirable thing to look at or smell, so I feel a little underdressed and vulnerable without something to cover them up. I think that was the point God was making with Moses. Removing his sandals forced Moses to relinquish his rights and control to God.

Taking off shoes was a custom in ancient Israel. Ruth 4:7 says, "Now in earlier times in Israel, for the redemption and transfer of property to become final, one party took off his sandal and gave it to the other. This was the method of legalizing transactions in Israel."

They would take off a sandal to relinquish control of something. That's why verse 8 says, "So the guardian-redeemer said to Boaz, 'Buy it yourself.' And he removed his sandal." If you know the story of Ruth, the kinsman-redeemer relinquished his responsibility for Ruth and gave it to Boaz. Taking off one's shoes was symbolic of giving up control.

Worship leaders are not in the business of guilt-tripping anyone into participating, because forced or coerced worship is not really worship. Instead, our goal is to help free people to worship God according to what is already in their hearts. If your heart is telling you to relinquish control by taking off your shoes while you stand on his holy ground, you are welcome to do so. But what is far more important than any outward expression of worship is that you become vulnerable and humble before our God.

Removing your shoes is just an outward expression of this inward humility.

Transition Through Reflection...

What are some things you own that you would consider holy or set apart?

1. _____

2. _____

3. _____

4. _____

5. _____

How does it make you feel when someone else uses them, particularly in a way in which they were not intended? Why?

_____

_____

Read 1 Peter 1:13–21. In verse 16, Peter quotes Leviticus 11:44, where God commands his people to be holy. From what you have read in this worship exercise, what is God really saying when he commands us to be holy?

_____

_____

What are some areas of your life that need to be set apart for the exclusive use of God alone?

1. _____

_____

2. _____

_____

3. _____

_____

4. _____

_____

5. _____

_____

Spend some time in prayer, declaring the holiness of God in your own words. Then confess the areas of your life that have not been set apart for God's exclusive use. Ask God to give you new desires and passions so that you may be holy as he commands.

Suggested Songs

Sing "Holy Is The Lord" by Chris Tomlin and Louie Giglio. You can also sing, "Revelation Song" by Jennie Lee Riddle (popularized by Philips, Craig & Dean, and Passion); "How Great Is Our God" by Chris Tomlin, Ed Cash, and Jesse Reeves; the hymn "Holy, Holy, Holy" by John Bacchus Dykes and Reginald Heber (Gateway Worship has a great version of this hymn); or "Holy Ground" by Geron Davis. (Chord charts are available at www.TransitionsWorship.com).

Taking God's Name In Vain

WHEN LEAH WAS pregnant with our fifth child, we had an ultrasound and found out we were having a boy. We shared the exciting news with our girls and then told the boys when they got home from school later that day.

The boys were really excited that we were having another boy until they heard the name we had picked out: Parker Jason.

"No fair!" yelled Gibson, who was eight.

Gibson has always been a daddy's boy. When he got hurt as a little kid, he would run to me for kisses. When he woke up scared in the middle of the night, he wanted Daddy, not Mommy. So, needless to say, I was glad to hear his response—not so much that he was jealous of the baby but that he wishes he had his daddy's name. Of course, Gibson is our ADD child, so we had to remind him that he *is* named after his daddy. His middle name is Bradford, which is my middle name. Once he heard this, Gibson let out a big, "Oh yeah."

As I thought about how excited Gibson would be to have my first name, I wondered, am I that excited to bear the name of my Father? How about you? Do you take that name seriously and try to bring honor to it? Or have you taken it for granted and maligned his name?

Do you count it a privilege to call yourself a Christian, to be called by the name of our Lord?

With his own finger, God gave us this command, "You shall not take the name of the LORD your God in vain." Most people assume this command simply means that we are not supposed to use God's name like a curse, something you utter when you hit your thumb with a hammer. Not all pastors or theologians will agree with me on this, but I believe this is not what the third commandment is about at all.

When God tells us not to take his name in vain, I believe he means that we should not call ourselves by his name if we do not mean it. We should not "take his name" (call ourselves Christians) "in vain" (if we live completely contrary to what that name is all about). Jesus said in Luke 12:10, "And everyone who speaks a word against the Son of Man will be forgiven…" The thieves on the cross both cursed Jesus. Matthew 27:44 says, "In the same way the robbers who were crucified with him also heaped insults on him." Did Jesus condemn these men? Did he rebuke them? No. In fact, as the hours passed, one of the thieves saw how Jesus endured the cross so completely different than him that it inspired him to place his faith in Jesus. Jesus made this promise to the thief: "Today you will be with me in paradise" (Luke 23:43).

On the other hand, the Pharisees—who held the expression of God's name in such high regard that they would not even utter it— were the very people of whom Jesus was most critical. Jesus called them a brood of vipers, whitewashed tombs, blind guides, hypocrites, and more. I believe Jesus had such harsh condemnation for these men, because they claimed to be followers of God but did not act on that claim.

In Revelation 3:15–16, Jesus says to the church in Laodicea, "I know your deeds, that you are neither cold nor hot. I wish you were either one or the other! So, because you are lukewarm—neither hot nor cold—I am about to spit you out of my mouth." Lukewarm Christians disgust Jesus. He is so repulsed that he would rather they be "cold" and not even confess to be Christians. Now *that* sounds like something so serious it would be included in the Ten Commandments.

Certainly, it is a sin to curse God's name, but it is much worse to call yourself by his name and not mean it. If you have been calling yourself a Christian but living a lukewarm life, take time to confess that to God.

Transition through Application...

Read 1 Peter 4:12–19. What does Peter say about bearing the name of Christ?

_____

_____

_____

Come up with five ways you can bear the name of Christ today.

1. _____

_____

2. _____

_____

3. _____

_____

4. _____
_____

5. _____
_____

Suggested Songs

Celebrate God's great mercy in granting you a new name by singing "Children of God" by Third Day (David Carr, Mac Powell, Mark D. Lee, Tai Anderson). You can also sing a song about your Father called "Forever Reign" by Jason Ingram and Reuben Morgan. The chorus says, "Oh, I'm running to Your arms—nothing compares to your embrace," and the bridge says, "My heart will sing, no other name, Jesus." "Carry Your Name" by Chris Tomlin, Christy Nockels, Jason Ingram, and Nathan Nockels; "I Glory In Your Cross," by Joel Engle; and the hymn "Take The Name Of Jesus With You" by Lydia Odell Baxter and William Howard Doane are also good songs to remind you of the new name that you have received through the sacrifice of our Lord Jesus. (Chord charts are available at www.TransitionsWorship.com).

50 DAYS OF WORSHIP

DAY 47

You Are So Good To Me

A PHILOSOPHY OF WORSHIP growing in many churches today promotes the idea that complex songs are "deep worship" and simple songs are "shallow worship." As a worship pastor, this perspective saddens me. I believe that we can benefit greatly from simple as well as the complex songs. If the lyrics are based on Scripture, then I do not believe it is a matter of depth versus shallowness. If the lyrics are Scriptural, then they are certainly deep. Instead, it is a matter of breadth. Is the song narrow or wide?

Worship songs that cover a vast array of themes should be labeled "wide," and lyrics that deal with a single theme or a few themes should be labeled "narrow." I believe that both types of worship songs should be utilized in our churches.

"You Are So Good To Me" by Ben Pasley, Don Chaffer, and Robin Pasley of Waterdeep (popularized by Third Day) is one worship song that has been criticized as "shallow." I disagree with that assessment. This song has a narrow focus, but it teaches us something very important

I hope that worship leaders and pastors will change their vocabulary from "deep" versus "shallow" to "wide" versus "narrow," because God's Word is not shallow, and neither are worship songs that are based on the depth of God's Word.

about worship. The phrases in this song are obviously metaphors for the Father, the Son, and the Holy Spirit. Scripture contains many metaphors for Jesus. In fact, Jesus assigned many to himself. For example, he said, "I am the bread of life" (John 6:35), "I am the light of the world" (John 8:12), "I am the gate" (John 10:9), "I am the true vine" (John 15:1), and "I am the good shepherd" (John 10:11). Not only did Jesus initiate some of these metaphors, his worshippers have applied their own metaphors for God throughout the Psalms. "You are my rock and my fortress… you are my refuge" (Psalm 31:3–4), "You are my portion" (Psalm 119:57), and "you are a shield around me" (Psalm 3:3).

When the author of Hebrews calls Jesus the "great Shepherd of the sheep," that was very meaningful to his first century audience. But how many of us have ever seen a shepherd? We know what a shepherd is, but we need an historian to explain to us the importance of shepherds and what this metaphor really meant to the people of the first century.

When Ben Pasley, Don Chaffer, and Robin Pasley wrote, "You Are So Good To Me," they wanted to use some new metaphors that would be relevant to our culture. "You are my strong melody." God is to the worshipper what a strong melody is to the songwriter. This is actually a biblical metaphor. Exodus 15:2 says, "The Lord is my strength and my song." The second part of the bridge says, "You are my dancing rhythm." To a dancer, nothing is more important than rhythm, just as nothing is more important to the saved than a Savior.

"You are my perfect rhyme." Rhyme is essential to the poet, just as the Holy Spirit is essential to our spiritual growth. All of these are deep metaphors to someone living in the 21ˢᵗ century, because we connect with this imagery. Music, dance, and poetry are near to the heart of most worshippers. These concepts may be simple, but they are not simplistic.

Transition Through Reflection...

Write your own metaphors for God. Use this sentence to help get you started: "God, you are to me as..." or "God, you are like..."

To spur some ideas, think about your profession and some of the tools that are essential to your work. What is important to you in life? What is essential to a relationship that is dear to you or your favorite hobby? As a musician I would describe the Trinity as a flawlessly tuned guitar. I like this metaphor of the unity that is found within the Trinity and the unity that we should have as the body of Christ. If this is a difficult exercise for you, remind yourself that worship should be costly and give it your best. If this is an easy exercise, then develop a few metaphors and maybe you can turn them into your own poem or song.

1. _____

2. _____

3. _____

4. _____

5. _____

Suggested Songs

If you are familiar with the song "You Are So Good To Me," take three minutes to sing through the simple lyrics. If you do not know the song, speak the lyrics to God as an expression of worship (Chord charts and lyrics are available at www.TransitionsWorship.com).

50 DAYS OF WORSHIP

Apple Of My Eye

PARKER JASON WAS born the day after our anniversary. Even though he is our fifth child, the pregnancy and anticipation of his birth was no less exciting than our other four. We eagerly anticipated Parker's arrival. Because of possible complications, we had four or five ultrasounds. It is so neat to be able to see your baby before he is born. Of course, all the women in our family looked at the images and commented that he was so cute. Not me.

"I don't know what you ladies are talking about," I said. "Frankly, the ultrasound photos frighten me. My baby looks like a skeleton, and I'm just hoping he doesn't look like that when he comes out!"

Looking at an ultrasound is not the same as rocking your baby in your arms and staring into his big, blue eyes. Sometimes I will walk in the room as my wife is holding Parker and just stare into his eyes, gazing at this miracle. But the ultrasound increased our anticipation to meet Parker face to face.

A friend of mine from church who is in the military was shipped out to Kuwait for a year. Due to security concerns, he could not even tell his wife when he would return, so she did not find out his ETA until one week prior to his arrival. It is difficult to imagine being separated from my wife and family for an entire year. Can you imagine how excited my friend was to see his wife again?

Take a few seconds to try and visualize that kind of excitement, to return from the battlefield and see your bride or husband again. I believe that Jesus feels this same kind of excitement as he anticipates returning for his church! Just as my friend cannot tell his wife when he will return, we do not know the day or the hour of Jesus' return, but we can be sure he will come for us, and that he will be overwhelmed with joy when we are finally reunited.

Jesus said, "Greater love has no one than this, that he lay down his life for his friends" (John 15:13). There is no greater love than Jesus' love for you. He could not possibly think more highly of you. He is thrilled to know you. He is electrified by the thought of you. You are perfect in God's eyes, because Jesus paid for your sins on the cross, and there's nothing you can do to make him love you any more or any less.

Transition Through Reflection...

In Psalm 17:8 David says, "Keep me as the apple of your eye; hide me in the shadow of your wings." What is the "apple of your eye?" Find a partner, get uncomfortably close to him or her, and then look into the person's eyes. As you stare into your partner's eyes, what do you see?

If you are alone, wait on this exercise until you can meet up with a loved one. Don't read ahead until you have an answer. The apple of the eye is when you look closely into someone's eye and you see your own reflection. David says that he is the apple of God's eye. David is the reflection in God's eye, which means God was looking intently at David, because he loves him so much.

You are the apple of God's eye, too. He loves you so much that he gazes at you like a mom looking with amazement at her newborn baby or like a soldier coming home from war and staring into the eyes of his love.

God wrote you a love letter—the Bible—so spend some time reading his Word today. On a separate piece of paper write, "How he Loves Me" and then read Ephesians 1. Make a list of the things that God says about you in this chapter and then hang your list on the refrigerator. Thank God for his incomprehensible love for you.

When you look into the eyes of the God who created and redeemed you, you will find that he has always been staring back at you.

Suggested Songs

Sing "As The Deer" by Martin Nystrom and focus on the third verse that says, "You alone are the real joy giver and the apple of my eye." Think about God's affection for you. Let his love capture your heart in this moment and sing these words back to the God who loves you more than you realize. If God is the apple of your eye, then he is the one you cherish above all others.

You can also sing "Captivate Us" by Charlie Hall, Christy Nockels, and Nathan Nockels; "Who Am I" by Mark Hall of Casting Crowns; "Beautiful One" by Tim Hughes (popularized by Jeremy Camp); or the hymn "One Day (Glorious Day)" by Charles Howard Marsh and John Wilbur Chapman. (Jeff Johnson and Casting Crowns have good versions of this hymn). (Chord charts are available at www. TransitionsWorship.com).

50 DAYS OF WORSHIP

DAY 49

Stimulating Our Senses

IN EPHESIANS 1:17−9, Paul prayed that our hearts would be enlightened:

> I keep asking that the God of our Lord Jesus Christ, the glorious Father, may give you the Spirit of wisdom and revelation, so that you may know him better. I pray that the eyes of your heart may be enlightened in order that you may know the hope to which he has called you, the riches of his glorious inheritance in his holy people, and his incomparably great power for us who believe.

Our brains sense changes in stimuli even more than the stimuli itself. If something touches your skin, you will notice it at first but if it continues, you will notice it less and less until it is removed and then you will notice it again. The same thing happens with background noises, sights, smells, and your mom's voice when she calls your name. That's why people who live in farm country can't smell what's all around them even though it's so obvious to everyone else the moment they step out of the car for a visit in the spring.

As an example of how this works, stare at the four dots in the middle of the image below for thirty seconds (try not to blink) and then close your eyes.

When you closed your eyes, what did you see? We have no idea what Jesus actually looks like, but this is a typical artist's rendering of him. The point of this exercise is not to impress you with an optical illusion; I want you to understand why this phenomenon occurs. When we stare at something for a while and then close our eyes, we see the negative image. The retinal cells in our eyes respond less and less the longer we stare at an image, sending a weaker signal to the brain. So when we close our eyes, those colors are still turned down by our brain, which makes the other colors seem brighter. This produces what looks like a negative image.

The same thing occurs in our spiritual lives unless we do something to stimulate our senses. The longer you are exposed to something, the more it fades into the background, even spiritually. This is one reason why so many Christians who were raised in church take Jesus for granted.

What have you been doing to stimulate your worship of God lately? Do you keep doing the same things over and over so that your senses begin to dull, or are you willing to change so that your relationship with God is renewed and refreshed? The whole idea of this devotional book is to stimulate your senses so you can renew your worship.

Isaiah 6:3 says, "Holy, holy, holy is the Lord Almighty; the whole earth is full of his glory." The longer we stare at the revelation of his glory, the less we notice it—unless the stimulus changes. Sometimes we fall back into that and our hearts are darkened. Today, you can stimulate your faith in a new way. Listen to Romans 1:20–21:

The whole earth is full of God's glory. All around us we should see God's glory, so why don't we notice it?

> For since the creation of the world God's invisible qualities—his eternal power and divine nature—have been clearly seen, being understood from what has been made, so that people are without excuse. For although they knew God, they neither glorified him as God nor gave thanks to him, but their thinking became futile and their foolish hearts were darkened.

Transition Through Reflection...

Read Psalm 19. Make a list of things in your house or outside the window that you have overlooked this week that display God's glory. How does that person, place, or thing display God's glory?

1. _____

_____

2. _____

3. _____

4. _____

5. _____

6. _____

7. _____

8. _____

9. _____

Suggested Songs

Spend a few minutes praising God in your own words for the displays of his glory that you just noticed. Then Sing "Open My Eyes" by Braden Lang and Reuben Morgan of Hillsong as you prepare yourself to have your heart stimulated in a new way so that the eyes of your heart may be enlightened. You can also sing "Open The Eyes of My Heart" by Paul Baloche; "Open Up Our Eyes" by Chris Brown, London Gatch, Mack Brock, Stuart Garrard, and Wade Joye of Elevation Worship; "Open Our Eyes Lord" by Bob Cull; or the hymn "To God Be The Glory" by Fanny Jane Crosby and William Howard Doane. (Chord charts are available at www.TransitionsWorship.com).

DAY 50
Pavlov's Dogs

WE ARE CERTAINLY creatures of habit. My wife and I live in the northeast, which was hit by super storm Sandy in the fall of 2012. Thankfully, we did not have any problems with flooding or damage from fallen trees, but we did lose power for seven days. Throughout the week, I walked around my house flipping light switches on, even though I was fully aware we had no electricity. I am so accustomed to flipping light switches on and off all day that I could not stop myself from doing so during the outage. But that's far from my only habit.

During college, I lived in a dorm room that had a community bathroom. Approximately twenty guys shared the same bathroom for an entire year. Thankfully, we were not required to clean the bathroom ourselves, so it did actually get cleaned a few times per week. However, neither the quality nor the quantity of the sanitation would have met the standards of my grandmother, who was responsible for cleaning the bathroom that we shared at home. Therefore, I developed an interesting habit. Any time I was in the bathroom, I would stand or walk on the sides of my feet. I didn't realize I was doing this, but I guess, subconsciously, I wanted as little of my feet touching the dirty floor as possible.

This habit was so ingrained in me throughout the course of my college career that more than 18 years later, I continue to stand on the sides of my feet while I am in my bathroom at home. Any time my wife sees me doing this; she is offended, because she assumes I am making a statement about the cleanliness of our bathroom. But I am simply a creature of habit, and I have no idea that I am still standing like that.

Pavlov would have had a field day conducting experiments on me. In case you don't remember, Pavlov was famous for the conditioned reflex experiments that he performed on dogs. Pavlov rang a bell before giving the dogs a meal, and the dogs would salivate. He did this over and over again, and then he took the food out of the equation. He rang the bell by itself, and the dogs still salivated. This is exactly what happened in my "formative" bathroom experience at college.

The nature of your bathroom conditioning is usually pretty inconsequential, but conditioning can be very destructive to the quality of your worship. Usually when you enter church and hear the music, you respond by worshiping God and getting a good feeling. This happens over and over until one day you walk into church, hear the music, and get a good feeling without pausing to worship.

Music should not be the stimulus to go vertical. God is the stimulus, and worship is our total response to God in faith.

I hope the one thing you have come to understand from reading this book is that worship is so much bigger than singing a few songs on Sunday morning. When we relegate worship to one day per week and limit our worship to music, it is easy to bypass the actual worship and focus on what we enjoy instead of honoring God. Throughout this book, I have provided suggestions for worship songs you can sing to God. However, don't just go through the motions of worship; engage your mind and your emotions in declaring God's worth without music today. Today, I want you to use your God-given creativity to think of a way to worship God without using music. That's why I haven't suggested any songs for this final devotion.

Transition through Application...

My final assignment for you is to purchase a small notebook to use as a praise journal. My wife picked up small notebooks that even had scripture verses about worship on the cover and put them in our Easter baskets this year. Try to find something like that or just use a plain notebook and design your own cover. Use the notebook as a praise journal and add new praises to the journal every day. Lamentations 3:22–23 says, "The faithful love of the Lord never ends! His mercies never cease. Great is his faithfulness; his mercies begin afresh each morning." We have new reasons to praise God each day, so I encourage you to think of something to write in your journal, because God is worthy of worship that is costly.

My hope is that this book has inspired you to make worship a part of your daily life. Please do not let that end with the completion of this book. If this book helped you to connect with God in a deeper way, would you consider paying it forward? Is there a friend or family member who would benefit from *Transitions* as you did? Please feel free to copy a relevant chapter and e-mail it to a friend or share one of the worship ideas with another worshipper who is in transition. Take five minutes now before you move on to the other busyness of your day and share the gift of worship!

ACKNOWLEDGEMENTS

Thank you to my team of unofficial editing friends and family: Marge Buyce, Merry Evans, Joe Forrest, Chip Hard, Karen Hard, Bonnie Heim, Leah Heim, and Tyler Stanhope. Thank you for the wonderful ideas on how to improve this project!

Thank you to my editor Kevin Miller for utilizing your many years of experience to provide helpful suggestions and thoughtful insights in order to put the finishing touches on this book.

Thank you to my interior designer Stephanie Anderson and Jera Publishing for providing a unique, fresh look for this project.

Thank you to my parents Jerry and Bonnie Heim for training me in the way I should go and showing me from childhood what it looks like to be a true worshipper of Jesus. Thank you to my brother Jared, my sister Vanessa, and their families for their love and support.

Thank you to everyone at The Narrow Road Church for adopting us into your family and for your example of telling others that God wants to adopt them into his family. Thank you to Mike Jarrell, my partner in ministry and friend for believing in me and encouraging me throughout my "Transition."

Thank you to my amazing wife Leah who inspires me to draw close to Jesus through her daily example. I continually find you sitting at Jesus' feet, and I am so glad to run this race with you by my side.

In Ecclesiastes 1:9, King Solomon said, "What has been will be again, what has been done will be done again; there is nothing new under the sun." Hence, it should come as no surprise that much of the material in this devotional was gleaned from the teaching and example of others. In writing this material over the last eighteen years, I was inspired by an untold number of books, sermons, seminars, worship services, and Internet blogs, so many more theologians, pastors, and worship leaders deserve credit for the ideas herein.

Finally, thank you to my Lord and Savior Jesus Christ who, in his mercy, is willing to accept my worship.

ABOUT THE AUTHOR

Jason Heim is on staff at the Narrow Road Church in Enola, Pennsylvania serving in church multiplication ministries. Jason and his wife Leah, with their six children, lead a Missional Community at their home in Levittown, Pennsylvania and are promoting Missional Ministry through the Evangelical Free Church of America. Jason served as a youth and worship pastor for 18 years. Jason graduated from Messiah College where he majored in Speech Communications and minored in Church Music. He received his Masters of Divinity from Bethel Seminary of the East.

If you would like more information on Transitions or how to invite Jason to speak at your church or event, please visit www.transitionsworship.com or reach out to Jason through jasonheim@ymail.com.

19723419R00179

Made in the USA
Middletown, DE
01 May 2015